Elements in Ancient and Pre-modern Economies
edited by
Kenneth G. Hirth
The Pennsylvania State University
Timothy Earle
Northwestern University
Emily J. Kate
University of Vienna

PEASANT ECONOMIES AND SOCIETIES IN ANCIENT ROMAN IBERIA

Jesús Bermejo Tirado
Universidad Carlos III de Madrid

Ignasi Grau Mira
Universidad de Alicante

Shaftesbury Road, Cambridge CB2 8EA, United Kingdom

One Liberty Plaza, 20th Floor, New York, NY 10006, USA

477 Williamstown Road, Port Melbourne, VIC 3207, Australia

314–321, 3rd Floor, Plot 3, Splendor Forum, Jasola District Centre, New Delhi – 110025, India

103 Penang Road, #05–06/07, Visioncrest Commercial, Singapore 238467

Cambridge University Press is part of Cambridge University Press & Assessment, a department of the University of Cambridge.

We share the University's mission to contribute to society through the pursuit of education, learning and research at the highest international levels of excellence.

www.cambridge.org
Information on this title: www.cambridge.org/9781009611213

DOI: 10.1017/9781009611190

© Jesús Bermejo Tirado and Ignasi Grau Mira 2025

This publication is in copyright. Subject to statutory exception and to the provisions of relevant collective licensing agreements, no reproduction of any part may take place without the written permission of Cambridge University Press & Assessment.

When citing this work, please include a reference to the DOI 10.1017/9781009611190

First published 2025

A catalogue record for this publication is available from the British Library

ISBN 978-1-009-61121-3 Hardback
ISBN 978-1-009-61123-7 Paperback
ISSN 2754-2955 (online)
ISSN 2754-2947 (print)

Cambridge University Press & Assessment has no responsibility for the persistence or accuracy of URLs for external or third-party internet websites referred to in this publication and does not guarantee that any content on such websites is, or will remain, accurate or appropriate.

For EU product safety concerns, contact us at Calle de José Abascal, 56, 1°, 28003 Madrid, Spain, or email eugpsr@cambridge.org

Peasant Economies and Societies in Ancient Roman Iberia

Elements in Ancient and Pre-modern Economies

DOI: 10.1017/9781009611190
First published online: September 2025

Jesús Bermejo Tirado
Universidad Carlos III de Madrid

Ignasi Grau Mira
Universidad de Alicante

Author for correspondence: Jesús Bermejo Tirado, jbtirado@hum.uc3m.es

Abstract: This Element revisits the historiographical and archaeological paradigms of Roman rural economies, with a particular focus on the peasant communities of Roman Iberia. Traditionally overshadowed by the dominance of the *villa schiavistica* model, which centers on large-scale slave-operated agricultural estates, recent interdisciplinary research has unveiled the complexity and persistence of peasant economies. By integrating data from archaeological surveys, rescue excavations, and textual analyses, this volume highlights the significance of dispersed settlements, small-scale farms, and sustainable agrarian strategies that defined the peasant landscape. Case studies from diverse sectors of the Iberian Peninsula demonstrate diverse modes of land use, such as intensive cultivation, crop rotation, and manuring, which contrast with the economic assumptions tied to elite-dominated production models. Furthermore, the authors explore Roman peasants' socioeconomic structures and adaptive strategies, emphasizing their pivotal role in shaping landscapes. This Element advocates for reexamining Roman peasantries as active and complex agents in ancient history.

Keywords: Roman archaeology, peasant studies, ancient economies, landscape archaeology, Roman social history

© Jesús Bermejo Tirado and Ignasi Grau Mira 2025

ISBNs: 9781009611213 (HB), 9781009611237 (PB), 9781009611190 (OC)
ISSNs: 2754-2955 (online), 2754-2947 (print)

Contents

1 Introduction: Defining Roman Peasant Economics 1

2 Roman Peasant Settlements and Productive Structures 9

3 Roman Peasant Economy as Seen through Landscapes and Agrarian Systems 31

4 Roman Peasant Networks and Economic Hubs 40

5 Peasant Economies and Roman Markets 45

6 Conclusions and Future Directions 48

   References 53

1 Introduction: Defining Roman Peasant Economics

In 1979, Prof. Peter Garnsey published an article in the *Proceedings of the Cambridge Philological Society,* in which he attempted to answer the question of why archaeologists and ancient historians had not studied peasant communities in Roman Italy. According to Garnsey, this gap was due to the negative response that preceding historiography had given to a previous question, "Did peasant proprietors survive in significant numbers in the Late Republic and Early Empire?" Despite Garnsey's own attempts (1976, 1980) and those of other notable scholars (Frayn 1974, 1979; Evans 1980, 1980b; Foxhall 1990; De Ligt 1990, 1991) to initiate a research focus on rural *proletarii*, non-slave laborers, smallholders, and rural tenants during the Roman period, this line of study remained stagnant until relatively recently. Several factors may explain the lack of continuity in this research. One of them is the undeniable academic success of the *villa schiavistica* model as a manifestation of the slave-owning mode of production in the Roman period, bolstered by the publication of the results of the archaeological excavations directed by Andrea Carandini (1985, 1989) of the Roman *villa* of Settefinestre in Etruria. The authority conferred by the vast majority of ancient historians on a relatively small group of sources (known as the *De Re Rustica* treatise writers, vid. Martin 1971) led to widespread acceptance of the idea of a progressive replacement of the traditional Republican-period, citizen-peasant communities by a model structured around the *villa* as a center of large slave holdings.

The extension of this agricultural production model, based on the *villa schiavistica* as the essential nucleus of the economic structure of other provincial territories, has been called "agrarian Romanisation" (Leveau 2014). It was understood as a natural result of the imperialist expansion of the Roman state throughout the Mediterranean (Remesal 2008). In this way, the archaeological concept of the *villa* was established as a material correlate of the Roman slave-owning production mode and the backbone of social and economic life in the rural world of large sectors of the Empire.

A paradigm shift has occurred in recent decades, however, thanks mainly to the development of survey projects carried out in Roman Italy and the systematic examination of data resulting from rescue archaeology. In view of all this evidence, it is no longer possible to sustain the idea that peasant communities disappeared during the late Republican and early Imperial periods (Launaro 2011; Bowes 2020). The traditional model is no longer useful to explain the complex configuration of Roman rural landscapes from a microregional perspective.

An increasing number of interdisciplinary projects is now responsible for giving visibility to the presence and relevance of various modes of occupation and exploitation of rural areas in the Roman world that foregrounds peasants from the perspective of anthropological peasant studies discussed next.

Archaeological analysis of peasant communities in Roman times involves a series of historiographical questions that transcend the lack of material evidence or textual sources. As various anthropologists (Wolf 1966: 13–17; Shanin 1971a: 15; Mintz 1973; Elis 1988b: 5–6) have pointed out, the subaltern nature of peasant communities throughout history has often hampered their ability to transmit or codify forms of social or cultural identity that are distinguishable from those of elite or aristocratic groups. These difficulties are reflected in the intense debates that have taken place within peasant studies since the inception of modern sociology (Edelman 2013). Nevertheless, it is possible to find generic characteristics for the concept of peasantry, in which to insert a large number of the social groups that populated the Roman countryside. A useful definition of the peasantry was proposed by Theodor Shanin in one of his most famous works *Peasantry: Delineation of a Sociological Concept and Field of Study*. He considers that the peasantry "consists of small agricultural producers who, with the help of simple equipment and the labor of their families, produce mainly for their own consumption and for the fulfilment of obligations to the holders of political and economic powers" (Shanin 1971a: 2, 3). However, as Shanin (1971b: 292) himself acknowledges, attempts to reduce the concept of peasantry to a closed social category would be a self-defeating exercise in reductionism for any social scientist or historian.

In light of all this new information and inspired by the line of research initiated by various scholars, the intention of this Element is to take up the question posed by Peter Garnsey for Roman Italy and to transfer it to the specific context of Roman Iberia (Table 1). To achieve this, the aim is to summarize recent publications regarding the study of archaeological evidence generated by various projects that have applied various survey and remote-sensing methodologies or have examined data generated by rescue archaeology projects. This is complemented by a review of extensive archaeological data contained in publications oriented according to traditional historiographical perspectives and legacy data. The discussion of all this information allows us to characterize the population structures of these rural communities on two fundamental levels. First, we examine the various territorial implantation and landscape configuration dynamics, in which these peasant communities are recorded in different micro-regions of the Iberian Peninsula. Second, we characterize the dwellings of these communities who lived outside (or rather on the margins of) the monumental *villae*. The purpose of this study is to analyze to what extent the landscape configuration, population structure, and economic and social life of various rural sectors of Roman Spain were conditioned by these peasant communities, by their ways of life, and by their forms of territorial exploitation.

Table 1 Summary of the main events and chronological periods mentioned in the text.

Period	Chronology	Key Events and Developments
Iron Age	c. 900 BC–218 BC	- Arrival of Indo-European and Eastern Mediterranean communities - Arise of Iberian and Celtiberian cultural groups - First cities-states in the Iberian Peninsula - Intensification of economy and increase of regional interchanges
Roman Conquest	218 BC–19 BC	- Progressive conquest in phases - Second Punic War (218–201 BC) - Wars with Iberian and Celtiberian communities. Numantine War (154–133 BC). - Roman territorial control mainly through local centers. - Augustus completes northern conquest
Early Roman Empire	1st century–3rd century	- Process of municipalization - Roman colonies established - Economic integration within Empire - Trade network development
Late Roman Empire	3rd century–5th century	- Crisis of the Roman Empire - Economic instability - Political fragmentation
Late Antiquity	AD 409–AD 711	- Collapse of Roman rule - Visigothic Kingdom of Toledo - Christianization of society - Islamic conquest

1.1 Roman Peasantry in the Textual Sources

A variety of Latin terms were used in various classical sources to designate diverse rural inhabitants in the Roman period: *rusticus* (Apul. *Metam*. XII. 24. 4), *rusticanus* (Cic. *Verr*. V. 34), *rusticulus* (Cic. *Sest*. XXXVIII. 82), *proletarius* (Aulus Gellius, *Noct. Att*. XVI. 10; Cic. *Res Publ*. II, 22, 10), *servus* (Juv. *Sat*. III, 9. 44), and *colonus*

(Cic. *pro Caec.* 57). However, there is no Latin word that can be used as an exact translation of the English word peasant. Many of these terms were used in various contexts to designate a wide variety of social realities, such as tenants, smallholders, rural workers, or even members of the local rural elites. However, in the entire history of Latin literature – at least that written up to the late Roman period – it is not possible to find a single source that describes individuals who can be identified as peasants. Despite the fact that some scholars have concerned themselves with analyzing the hidden transcripts contained in the work of some Latin authors, such as the writers of agricultural handbooks *De Re Rustica* (Kron 2017), Ovid's *Metamorphoses* (López Medina 2020), Pliny's *Natural History* (Shaw 2015: 278–279), or the *Epistles* of Dio Chrysostom (Erdkamp 2005: 55–105), it is almost impossible to find detailed and non-biased information about the worldview or the material living conditions of these groups in a review of literary sources.

Other textual sources offer more direct information about these communities during the Roman period: for example, the laws that regulated the great imperial domains of North Africa, such as the *lex Manciana* (Kehoe 1988; Kolendo 1991; De Ligt 1998) or the *lex Hadriana* (González Bordas 2020). These are known in great detail thanks to the study of inscriptions documented in various sectors of *Africa Proconsularis*. Other North African inscriptions, in particular, funerary texts, offer us access to other ideological references about the uses and customs of these peasant communities of Roman Africa. This is the case of the famous Maktar harvester inscription (*CIL*, VIII 11824; *ILS* 7457, for the best study published to date see Shaw 2015: 3–92, 281–298), as well as other lesser known inscriptions that contain biographical references to the concerns and virtues associated with these communities (Stone 1998). Other legal texts, such as leases or harvesting contracts for agricultural products (P. Sarap. 49 and 50; P. S. I. 789; P. Flor. 80 and 101; Montevecchi 1950), also offer us notable information on the living conditions of these sectors of rural society in the context of Roman Egypt (Bagnall 2005; Bowman 2009).

Although these sources contain interesting information about the economic conditions and social life of peasant communities in various provinces of the Roman Empire, in the specific context of Roman Iberia, with a few exceptions related to generic references to some rural settlements (Curchin 1985; Le Roux 2009) or certain onomastic or kinship references related to forms of dependency in rural contexts (Sastre 2007), we have practically no textual sources that contain references to these rural communities (Tarpin 2002). Similarly to North Africa, we have some epigraphic sources for the Iberian Peninsula that provide interesting evidence. This is the case with the bronze tablet containing the allocation of enclosure lots (*sortitio*) of *Ilici* (Elx, Alacant) (Mayer and Olesti 2001), an exceptional source that allows us to understand the allocation of small plots of land that were to be part of the centuriation of the territory of this Roman colony. This document serves to confirm that, at least at the time of the formal act of surrender or submission to Roman authority of the territory (*deditio*) and the ritual of foundation of a new Roman town (*deductio*), the Roman surveyors intended to establish a relatively equal distribution of small plots among the different veterans and coloners, who would then cultivate them using strategies similar to those of other smallholders in various historical contexts (especially Republican Italy). This tablet is an example of the detailed administrative record that Roman magistrates developed at a local level to ensure the effective implementation of taxation on all inhabitants of the countryside in provincial territories. Despite the importance of this source, to which we will return later, it remains one of the few textual sources that reference this type of smallholders in the context of the Iberian Peninsula. To a large extent, research on the living conditions and historical evolution of peasant communities from the Roman period in Iberia has to be limited fundamentally to the analysis of archaeological evidence. Thus, the main aim of this study is the construction of a historical portrait of the peasantries of Roman Iberia through the analysis of various (and dispersed) archaeological testimonies bequeathed to us by those communities.

1.2 Analyzing Peasant Economics in the Roman Period

The examination of Roman rural economies in recent decades has been predominantly shaped by the application of modern economic models. The classic debates between "modernists" and "primitivists" have now transitioned toward an emphasis on quantitative indicators and the legal-institutional framework (Kehoe 1988; Scheidel, Morris, and Saller 2007) to comprehend the ways in which community economic structures functioned. Many of these approaches stem from a liberal application of the market concept as the backbone of such analyses (Temin 2013). Even interpretations rooted in Marxist conceptions (e.g., the slave mode of production) of the *De Re Rustica* treatises and archaeological records from systematic excavations since the 1970s–80s are interwoven with this mercantilist or proto-capitalist perspective on the Roman economy (Carandini 1985; Leveau 2014; Launaro 2015). However, without dismissing the relevance of these approaches for understanding the Roman economy, it is crucial to acknowledge that such studies overshadow or disregard the economic constraints and motivations of a substantial portion of the Roman rural population.

As Chayanov (1925) previously established, the economy of peasant groups is structured by the need to navigate a series of decisions and balances that transcend the microeconomic conceptions of classical economic theory (Figure 1). This does not imply that this economy is simplistic or primitive, as

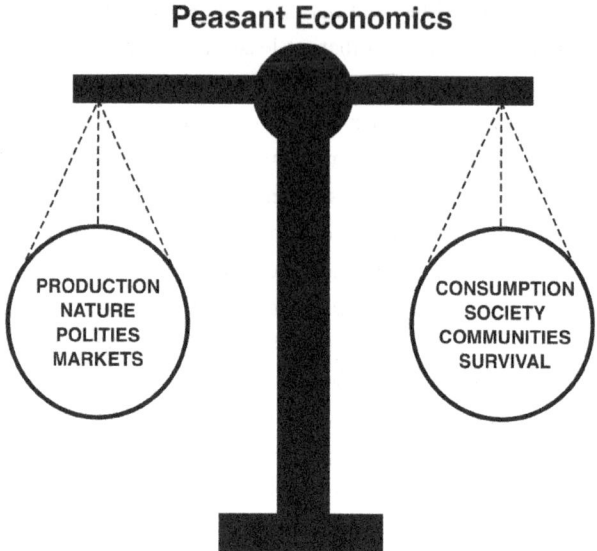

Figure 1 Graph of the main balances related to peasant economies' performance.

some contemporary scholars of the Roman economy may implicitly suggest. Nor is the wholesale disappearance of peasant communities in the Roman world due to the development of a mercantile economy reliant on massive slave labor, as has been claimed on various occasions. In the present era, marked by the global application of neoliberal paradigms, we have witnessed the emergence of new forms of the peasant economy and the reformulation of agricultural paradigms beyond capitalist conceptions (Van der Ploeg 2008). Therefore, the assertion of a complete substitution of the Roman peasantry as a collective historical agent is only plausible from an ideologically biased perspective of the ancient world as a necessary precursor to the capitalist economy of the contemporary world.

The analysis of peasant economies cannot be conducted solely through classical mercantile lenses. Theirs was an economy not based on the investment of past labor effort with wages (or the investment of financial resources in the purchase of slave labor). To sustain themselves, these peasant groups were predominantly reliant on work carried out by members of a family unit and other members of the extensive and complex corporate groups that were characteristic of preindustrial and other contemporary rural societies (Shanin 1990; Netting 1993). Building upon this initial premise, the following sections will explore the essential elements and balances that these rural communities of Roman Iberia had to maintain for their subsistence.

A fundamental balance in peasant economies exists between production and consumption, operating within an investment and subsistence framework (Halstead 2014). While diverging from modern financial economic models, these systems incorporate distinct forms of capital. In this context, "capital" encompasses tangible assets including farmsteads, cultivated fields, land improvements, tools, and productive infrastructure (Van der Ploeg 2008: 45). These elements often generate substantial material remains, providing archaeologists with valuable data for characterizing the various sorts of "capital" available to Roman-era rural settlements across the Iberian Peninsula. The second section of this Elements project aims to provide an updated overview of our current understanding of this material evidence, which serve to characterize the various forms of "capital" available to farms and other forms of rural habitation during the Roman period across different regions of the Iberian Peninsula.

Another balance that every peasant economy must address concerns the relationship between the natural and the social spheres (Toledo 1990). The agricultural and livestock activities of these communities are invariably structured through specific interventions in or exploitation of the landscape. Contrary to the common perception of the relative simplicity of peasant life, these communities were in fact characterized by the development and implementation of diverse agricultural strategies linked to various cultivation and husbandry methods across different environmental contexts. This entails the application of multiple approaches to exploiting and modifying the neighboring landscapes. In the case of peasant communities, this capacity to alter the surrounding landscapes is not primarily based on potential profit. Consequently, peasant groups may develop agricultural strategies such as intensification, where the production of short-term yields is so marginal that it would be automatically discarded by any agricultural enterprise based on financial or capitalist calculations. Although these practices may not be optimal in terms of economic yields, they often ensure long-term sustainability. This balance is defined in terms of co-production – an ecological relationship between humans and nature (Chayanov 1925: 58; Gerritsen 2002, 2012; Altieri and Toledo 2011; Van der Ploeg 2008, 2015). In the third section, we will analyze the agricultural strategies deployed by peasant groups in different regions of Roman Iberia and the landscape alterations that these strategies entailed. As we shall see, diverse archaeological indicators suggest adaptations in the implementation of intensification agrarian strategies.

One fundamental aspect is related the operational framework of peasant groups to the mobilization of household labor. Relevant to this question is the structural relationship between operational models based on land quantity – depending on the availability of slave or dependent labor, as in the case of the *villa* system – and those limited by labor, characteristic of peasant economies. However, the restriction of household labor should offer the possibility of some flexibility through cooperation or collaboration between domestic units (Erdkamp 1999: 559–560). This collaboration in collective works could be expressed, as we will present, by evidence of fortified houses or landscape infrastructures.

Peasant settlements were not isolated entities. In many cases, they were subject to various relationships of dependence with respect to external powers and economic networks. In recent decades, numerous studies in the field of peasant studies have emphasized the need to analyze other external balances that these communities had to confront (Van der Ploeg 2008, 2015; Scott 2009; Narotzky 2016). One of these relates to forms of interaction established within these economies to articulate broader networks, referring to the creation of economic ties outside commercial markets. Often these networks were articulated through cultural and religious practices, which tended to serve as a pretext for the development of more or less informal economic practices. Although these inter-domestic networks are essential for understanding the economies of the ancient world (Hirth 2020: 43–75), we still lack many studies that analyze them in depth in the Roman period. In the fourth section of this Element, we will analyze how these communities articulated economic relationships and hubs on a local scale. Many of these peasant networks seem to be structured based on practices guided by the principles of a moral economy, intertwined with traditional cultural and religious practices rather than a conventional mercantilist intent.

Another external balance that these peasant settlements had to confront concerns their relationship with political powers and endogenous economic structures (Hobsbawm 1973; Wolf 1982; Scott 1998; Van der Ploeg 2015). Scholars need a better understanding of how empires organized and conquered territories and extract resources, while at the same time allowing for reasonable subsistence support of the conquered populations. Despite these settlements not being primarily focused on generating high yields, they were not entirely isolated from the economic networks established in the Mediterranean under Roman domination. In some cases, the Roman state itself acted as a direct manager of large economic concessions, as in the case of mining in certain areas of the peninsula, which profoundly affected the economic structures developed by peasant communities surrounding some cities or exploitation centers (Domergue 1990; Orejas and Sastre 1999). In the fifth section, we will analyze these influences, coercion, and the degree of integration of these peasant economies from various regions of Roman Iberia within the context of Roman economic networks at other macrospatial scales.

The analysis of archaeological evidence facilitates examination of the tactics employed by different peasant communities in addressing these balances. While precise quantitative analysis may not be feasible, comparative study demonstrates the variety and complexity of economic decisions that these groups faced. In some instances, their economic practices proved more sustainable than those of large Roman urban centers with their monumental infrastructures and extensive financial networks. This study aims to provide a refined analysis of these peasant economies, transcending traditional approaches to reveal the diversity of agrarian strategies developed in the rural areas of ancient Iberia during the Roman period.

2 Roman Peasant Settlements and Productive Structures

This section underscores dispersed peasant farmsteads in rural settlements and their role shaping the region's agricultural economy and social structure in Roman Iberia. One of the main reasons for the poor representation of peasant communities in past scholarship on Roman Spain is the widespread application of the archaeological concept of *villa* to designate the majority of the rural settlements documented on the Iberian Peninsula (on this question see Molina Vidal 2011; Fernández-Ochoa, Salido, and Zarzalejos 2014). The term *villa* is usually associated with settlements containing elements of a certain monumentality, as well as other decorative devices associated with prestigious consumption practices, such as mosaics and sculptural decoration. However, the disparity in the morphology, facilities, and scale of the rural settlements designated as such in much of the preceding bibliography (Gorges 1979; Fernández Castro 1982; Casas et al. 1995; Chavarría et al. 2006; Chavarría 2007; Teichner 2008; Fernández Ochoa, García-Entero, and Gil Sendino 2008; Fiches, Plana, and Revilla 2013; Hidalgo 2016; Martínez, Nogales, and Rodà 2020; D'Encarnaçao, Cardoso, and Almeida 2020) indicates that the application of this category does not necessarily correspond to specific architectural typology criteria. Rather, we are faced with an archaeological category generated from a biased reading of certain literary sources, such as the authors of works *De Re Rustica* or Vitruvius. However, the *villa* not only serves to designate an architectural model, but it is also usually associated with an economic model of agricultural exploitation linked to the slave mode of production (Remesal 2008). The generic use of this concept has implied the assumption of the slave mode of production as the predominant option for the social and economic structure of rural societies in the Roman world. This has contributed to increasing the opacity of peasant communities as an object of historiographical attention on the part of scholarship.

In the following section we shall review a set of rural habitat modes attested in recent decades in various regional contexts of the Iberian Peninsula. The objective is to give visibility to those architectural models that would have been occupied by the peasant communities of Roman Spain.

2.1 Farmsteads and Other Forms of Scattered Settlement

Whereas the *villa* concept has been used to designate a large number of diverse rural settlements, paradoxically in many publications dealing with the archaeology of the Roman rural Hispania a tendency can be detected that avoids the use of the term "farm" to designate humbler settlements. Despite presenting productive infrastructures related to the processing of agricultural yields, these sites cannot be linked to surplus production similar to that of the *villa schiavistica*. Instead, we see that ambiguous formulas such as "rural settlement," "rural establishment," or "agricultural building" are used in a way that is inversely proportional to the case of the *villa* concept. Behind this rejection of the use of the term "farm" lies its connection to modes of social organization and agricultural exploitation associated with peasant societies.

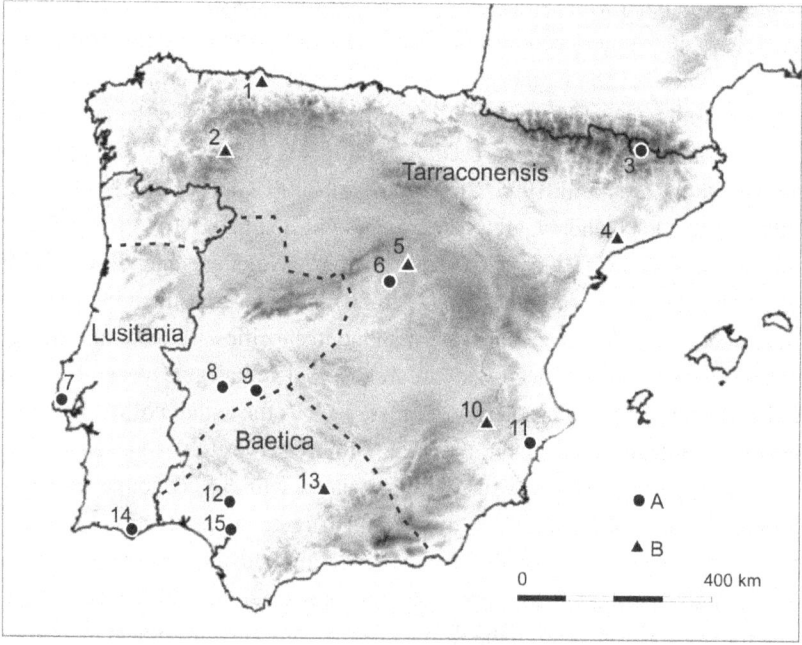

Figure 2 Map of the Iberian Peninsula with the location of the provincial demarcations established in the early Imperial period. (A) Peasant Farmsteads sites. (B) *Villae* with later phases of peasant occupation.

Different forms of dispersed habitat lie, we believe, behind these ambiguous terms that, for lack of a better term, could be called farms. The use of this designation should not be understood as an attempt to establish a specific architectural typology but as a term for a settlement linked to a family farm. This is regardless of the family's civic status or the legal regime of connection with land ownership and is different from the archaeological models clearly attributed to the *villa schiavistica*. This is the case, for example, with the farm documented at El Clot de Galvany (Elx, Alacant) (Figure 6: E) (Molina Vidal 2015). Located near wetlands in a marginal sector of its region, this settlement offered an archaeological context altered by the construction of a 16th-century chapel. Beneath that building, the remains of a square structure just over 20 m long were located. It consisted of two modules built of masonry walls with two façades bound with lime mortar and small stone fragments.

The first of these modules is composed of three rectangular rooms. It probably had porticoes, indicated by round stone base that would have acted as a base or support for wooden posts. In one room (Area 4), the remains of an irregularly shaped feature could be interpreted as a hearth and another feature related to household production (Molina Vidal 2015: Figure 5). The other module is made up of a single room (Area 7) with an elongated floor plan that could have been a storage room or shed attached to the house structures. The roof tiles found in abandonment levels of the structure, together with the range of pottery finds associated with these contexts (TSSG, ARS, Roman painted ware of Iberian tradition and African cooking ware, Molina Vidal 2015: 112), allow us to place the sequence of occupation of this settlement between the 1st and the end of the 3rd centuries AD.

Another example of a farmstead of these characteristics in the territory of *provincia Tarraconensis* is that documented in Zarzalejo (Arroyomolinos, Madrid) (Vigil-Escalera 2012: Figure 2; Bermejo Tirado 2017: 360–361) (Figure 3). It contains four different buildings arranged irregularly around a central open area, as well as a small square structure with one open side. The so-called Building 1 has a pool (*lacus*) for wine or olive-oil processing. In the adjoining room, which has the remains of waterproof paving, only one floor level was documented. Given its connection to the *lacus* and its raised elevation, it was probably used as a pressing facility. In the next room (Area 13), also part of Structure 1, the remains of a domestic hearth consisting of a brick surface supported by a mudbrick substructure were documented (Vigil-Escalera 2012: 168–169); a series of small postholes was found around this hearth.

In the southern sector of this site archaeologists excavated storage pits, pits for large containers (*dolia*), and rubbish dumps (Bermejo Tirado 2017: 361). In addition, they found a network of small-diameter postholes, probably related to

Figure 3 Plan of the Roman farmstead documented at El Zarzalejo (Arroyomolinos, Madrid), after Bermejo Tirado (2017).

the construction of wooden structures that could have been raised wooden silos similar to those found in different contexts of *Gallia Comata* (Ferdière 2015: Type 1; Martin 2019), or composite looms (a hypothesis already pointed out by Vigil-Escalera 2012: 169). The analysis of the pottery assemblages discovered inside allows us to propose an occupation sequence from the early 2nd century to the last third of the 3rd century AD (Vigil-Escalera 2012: 169). El Zarzalejo is not an isolated case in this central sector of Roman Spain. The intensive activity of preventive archaeology undertaken in the Madrid metropolitan area since the late 1990s has allowed the excavation of a large number of settlements of this type. Sites such as Tesoro de la Herradura (Fuente el Saz, Madrid) (Figure 4: A), Soto de Mozanaque (Algete, Madrid) (Figure 5: A), PGOU 9 (Torrejón de Velasco, Madrid) (Figure 4: B), site 10' of Tinto Juan de la Cruz (Pinto, Madrid) (Figure 5: C), and Val de la Viña (Alovera, Guadalajara) (Figure 4: C), among others (Bermejo Tirado 2017: 354–361), are examples of peasant dwellings with these characteristics in this rural sector of Roman Carpetania (Bermejo Tirado 2022).

Peasant Economies and Societies in Roman Iberia 13

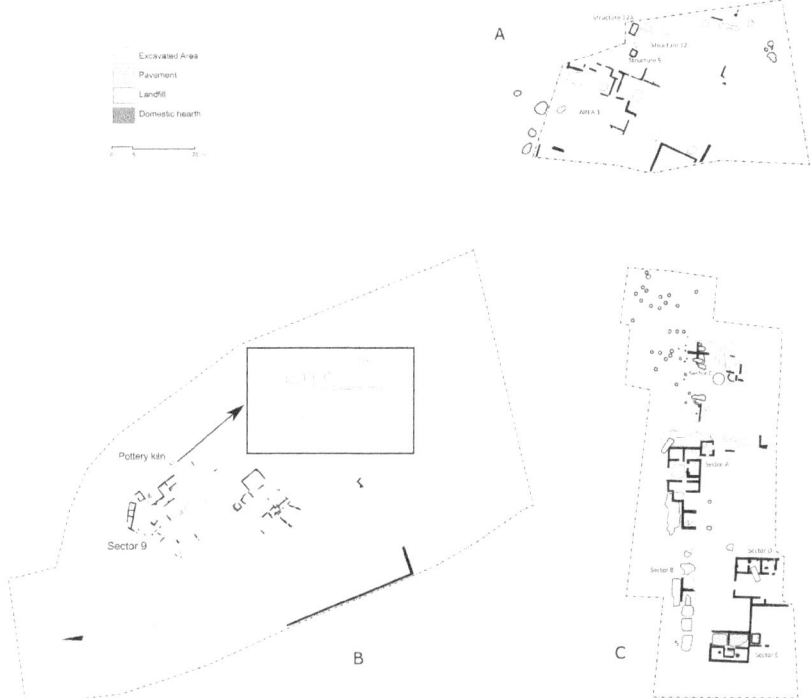

Figure 4 Some examples of Roman farmsteads documented in central Roman Spain. (A) Tesoro de la Herradura (Fuente el Saz, Madrid). (B) PGOU 9 Torrejón de Velasco (Madrid). (C) Val de la Viña (Alovera, Guadalajara), after Bermejo Tirado (2017).

Another peasant settlement with similar characteristics called Monte da Nora was in the western part of *Lusitania*, in the Alentejo (Terrungem, Sintra) (Teichner 2013: 145, Figure 5) (Figure 6: C). The second occupation phase of this settlement contains three architectural modules that date from the end of the 1st to the 3rd centuries AD (Teichner 2008: 67, Figures 12, 24–25). A first building located to the north of the complex appears to be a relatively humble structure made up of six quadrangular rooms just over 30 m long. Several features are documented to the south of this complex: some storerooms with cereal silos, a small shed for wine or olive pressing, and the remains of three kilns that appear to have been for firing common ware or tiles. All this equipment has been related to a peasant economy oriented toward subsistence or, in the case of the pottery kilns, to the production of surpluses for local markets.

The settlement known as Carrión was of a similar size in the territory surrounding *Augusta Emerita* (Mérida, Badajoz) (Figure 6: A). Although it

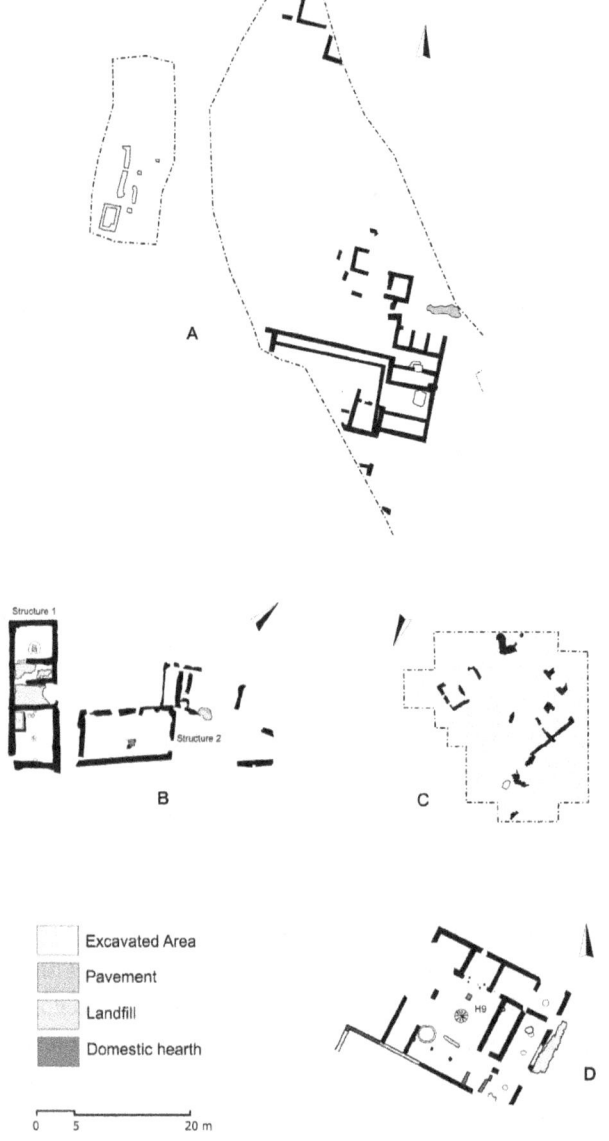

Figure 5 Some examples of Roman farmsteads documented in central Roman Spain. (A) Soto de Mozanaque (Madrid). (B, C) Tinto Juan de la Cruz 10' (Pinto, Madrid), after Bermejo Tirado (2017). (D) La Indiana (Pinto, Madrid), after Vigil-Escalera (2012).

was initially identified as a *villa* (Picado 2004), a subsequent study generically described it as an "agricultural building" (Sánchez Dámaso 2013: 297, Figure 3). This structure of early imperial date presents a single architectural module, with a length slightly greater than 30 m and a width of less than 20 m,

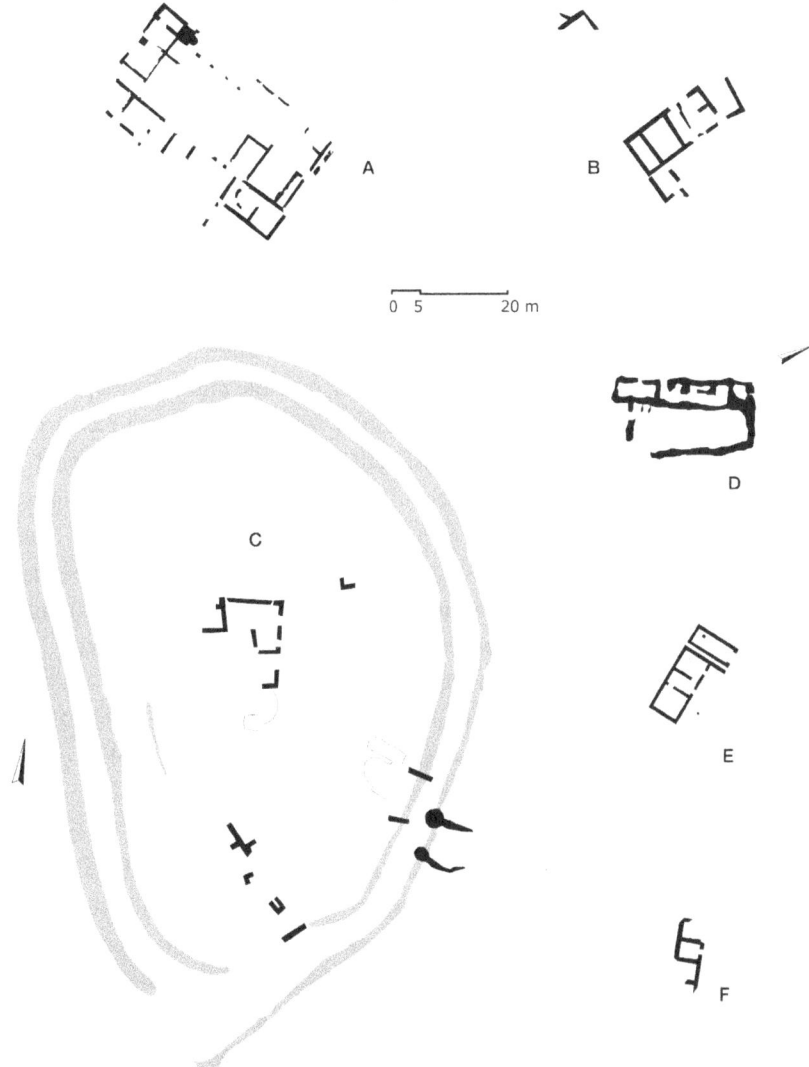

Figure 6 Some examples of Roman farmsteads documented in different areas of the Iberian Peninsula. (A) Carrión (Mérida, Spain), after Sánchez Barrero (2013). (B) El Chaparral I (Sevilla, Spain), after Fernández Flores and Carrasco Gómez (2013–2014). (C) Monte da Nora (Sintra, Portugal), after Teichner (2013). (D) Gallina Ahorcada (Sevilla, Spain), after Fernández Flores and Carrasco Gómez (2013–2014). (E) Cabezo-Clot de Galvany (Alacant, Spain), after Molina Vidal (2015). (F) Mermeleiros (Quarteira, Portugal), after Teichner (2013).

similar to that of other rural complexes documented at sites in the surroundings of *Emerita*, such as Villaemérita (Sánchez Dámaso 2013) and Cerro Gordo. The settlement in Carrión presents a grape press related to small-scale winemaking.

In the same space as the press, an elongated area with a row of central pilasters is found. It is interpreted as a small granary (*horreum*) probably used for cereal storage (Sánchez Barrero 2013: 297).

A rural settlement form, the so-called fortified houses, has attracted the attention of several researchers. One good example is El Castejon de Las Merchanas (Don Benito, Badajoz). This model of dispersed rural habitat is frequently documented in Portugal, although such settlements have also been found in the *Baetica* area. It is characterized by wide perimeter walls, sometimes built with Cyclopean masonry. This construction technique, together with the chronology of many of these settlements, mainly between the 2nd century BC and the turn of the era, has led to a possible military interpretation (for this discussion see Mayoral 2018; Moret 2016). In line with recent proposals, however, we agree that these settlements should be interpreted as fortified farms. They would have been inhabited by the first generations of settlers in territories some distance from the protection of a large military presence in late Republican Hispania. Their size, spatial distribution, and infrastructure match perfectly what could be expected of a family farming operation oriented toward subsistence in a territorial environment with little stability, such as southwestern Iberia in the Republican era.

In the context of *Baetica*, various rescue excavations in the Viar Valley (Sevilla) described several Roman-era farms similar to those described earlier. At one of these sites, known as Gallina Ahorcada (Figure 6: D), excavations documented several buildings probably linked to a small-scale agricultural operation. The most complex of these structures is the so-called Building 1 with masonry walls (Fernández Flores and Carrasco Gómez 2013–2014: 100, Figure 3) and some 23 m long by 12 m wide. It is a dwelling composed of a single module of five rooms connected to an open courtyard (Room 1) by a large entrance opening that could have served as a corral for domestic livestock (Fernández Flores and Carrasco Gómez 2013–2014: 101). The pottery contexts beneath the collapse of this phase do not allow a specific occupation chronology to be attributed to the site, beyond a generic range between the 2nd and 5th centuries AD. Particularly interesting among the finds in this building was a ploughshare, which allowed the inhabitants of this settlement to be linked to intensive cereal farming or horticulture. In the southern sector of this same settlement there are two more structures, each composed of a single freestanding room.

The aforementioned excavations also documented another similar settlement, El Chaparral I, composed of two buildings built with irregularly faced masonry plinths (Figure 6: B). Building 1 has a morphology and dimensions (19 x 14 m) similar to the structure described at Gallina Ahorcada. It is made up of seven rooms flanked by two slabs that paved the perimeter of the building on its longest sides. The so-called Room 5 of this building could also be identified as an open corral wall on its northern side. The finds beneath the collapse levels of this building allow us to assign an approximate chronology for the occupation of the settlement as between the 1st and the end of the 2nd centuries AD. In the northwestern corner of the settlement excavation area, another module consisted of a single rectangular room that would have served as a small storeroom or shed.

In the bordering municipality of Castilblanco de los Arroyos (Sevilla), these same rescue excavations revealed another similar settlement at the archaeological site of La Rivera (Fernández Flores and Carrasco Gómez 2013–2014: 115–117). In the second phase of this settlement, the best preserved, the remains of another rectangular dwelling with excavated dimensions of 19.45 x 11 m were found. As in the previous cases, the walls of this building were built with irregular masonry of different sizes. Furthermore, in a similar way to the other settlements in the middle course of the Viar River, the house in this phase of La Rivera was structured as five small rooms. In two of these, a hydraulic pavement and another ceramic tile floor were documented. These could be related to facilities for small-scale winemaking or olive oil processing. The most elongated rooms in the enclosure could be identified as storage spaces (Room 5) or domestic livestock corrals (Room 6) (Fernández Flores and Carrasco Gómez 2013–2014: Figure 14). The finds associated with their excavation can only be linked generically to a chronological framework situated between the 2nd and the beginning of the 5th centuries AD.

To conclude this review of the different types of dispersed peasant habitat documented in recent years on the Iberian Peninsula, we now refer to a series of settlements that would have been related to alternative forms of small-scale, traditional subsistence agriculture, with which these farms are usually linked.

This is the case of the settlement of Marmeleiros (Figure 6: F) located on the banks of the River Quarteira (Portugal), in the former territory of *Ossonoba* (Teichner 2008: 413–415). This farm, with a well-defined occupation from the turn of the era, was probably inhabited by a domestic group that would have alternated the exploitation of maritime resources with some intensive agriculture.

Another type of settlement important for the rural economy of certain mountainous areas of the Iberian Peninsula was the dispersed structures related to the practice of transhumance to exploit high-altitude forest resources. Knowledge of the management and uses of mountain areas in antiquity has been characterized by a historiographical gap that, in many cases, can be explained by the difficulty of undertaking research in such environments

(Leveau and Palet 2010). However, thanks to several recent interdisciplinary research projects, our knowledge of this mountain settlement during the Roman period has increased. It is worth highlighting the pioneering work carried out by the Institut Català d'Arqueologia Clàssica (ICAC) for understanding the high mountain Pyrenean landscapes during the Roman period.

A first microregional area studied by that group of researchers is located at the confluence of the Madriu-Perafita-Claror valleys in the Andorran Pyrenees. These projects allowed the excavation of several Roman-era habitations related to the exploitation of livestock in high mountain pastures at levels that had not been exploited previously (Palet et al. 2013: 338). The intensification of livestock farming in the Roman period is associated in these territories with the building of various shelters, enclosures and huts, which, thanks to the radiocarbon dating sequences obtained, have been unequivocally dated to the Roman period. This is the case with the enclosure (designated Structure M135) documented at the Basses de Setut III archaeological site (Figure 7: B). Thanks to the stratigraphic survey undertaken it can be dated to the 1st century AD (Palet et al. 2013: 338, Figure 4). Several huts at other sites, such as Planells de Perafita I and Pleta de les Bacives I, also have radiocarbon dating that allows periods of occupation in Roman times to be identified. Equally revealing in demonstrating the complexity of these pastoral practices are the milking corridor structures in the same region at Pleta de Claror I site (Colominas, Palet, and Garcia-Molsosa 2020) (Figure 7: A).

In a second micro-regional area, the Coma de Vaca valley, a rectangular-shaped shepherd's hut (Hut 114) was excavated (Figure 7: C). Measuring 5 x 4 meters, inside an occupation level from the Roman period was documented (UE 214-215), as well as finds associated with a context of between the second half of the 1st and the 3rd centuries AD. Whereas these sites can be related to various livestock practices, a third microregional area studied by the same group, the Serra de Cadí (Alt Urgell), presents features that denote a diversification of natural resource exploitation. These include, in addition to livestock, the exploitation of pine resin and charcoal and iron metallurgy (Palet et al. 2013: 335–336).

Although at a much lower altitude than these examples from the eastern Pyrenees, a rescue excavation carried out in the municipality of Artesa (Lleida) revealed another hut that could also be related to livestock exploitation in the territory of *Ilerda*: La Gravera de L'Eugeni (Lleida) (Morín et al. 2003) (Figure 7: D). At this site, the excavators found the remains of a cabin bottom directly cut in the calcareous gravel, to which the name of the place refers. The abundant pottery remains recovered in its fills, as well as in other deposits associated with an attached hearth, included various sherds of black glaze ware

Peasant Economies and Societies in Roman Iberia 19

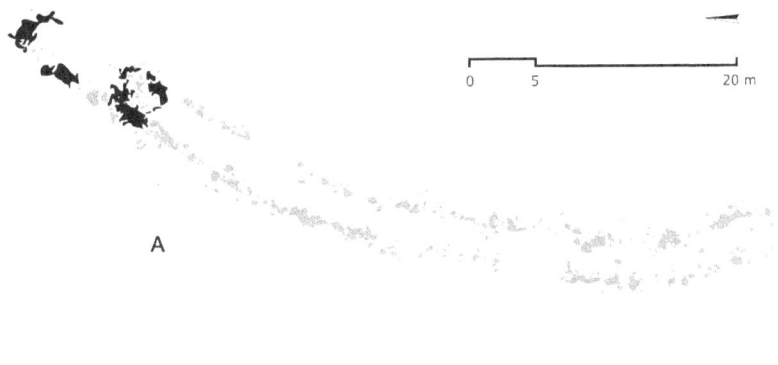

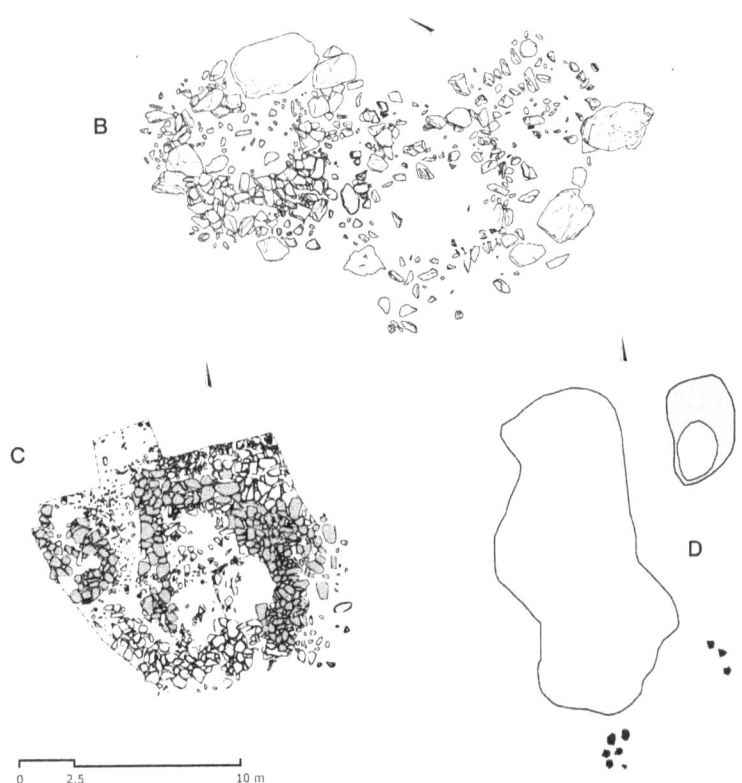

Figure 7 Some examples of Roman huts documented in different areas of the nordest Iberian Peninsula. (A). Schematic plan of the milking corridor recorded at Pileta del Claror I (Andorra), after Colominas, Palet, and Garcia-Molsosa (2020). (B) Structure M135 from Bases del Setut III, after Palet et al. (2013). (C) Hut 114 from Coma de Vaca (Andorra), after Palet et al. (2013). (D) Roman hut from La Gravera de L'Eugeni (Lleida), after Morín et al. (2003).

and TSH, allowing us to place the occupation of this settlement at between the 1st century BC and the 2nd century AD.

2.2 Dispersed Farmsteads and Villages from Surveys

Settlement structures can also be recorded by archaeological surface surveys. This is a fruitful way to recognize peasant occupations without costly excavations. For such an identification, it is necessary to apply the high-precision recording methods used in full coverage surveys; otherwise, these humble sites may go unnoticed. They take on the surface form of pottery and simple building remains, the concentration of which normally covers an area of approximately 500–800 m². This small size, together with utilitarian architectural forms, no conspicuous buildings and an absence of facilities for processing of large-scale agricultural productions are the defining features.

We have already mentioned the farm excavated at El Clot de Galvany in eastern Iberia. It has served as a model to define a series of points detected in the

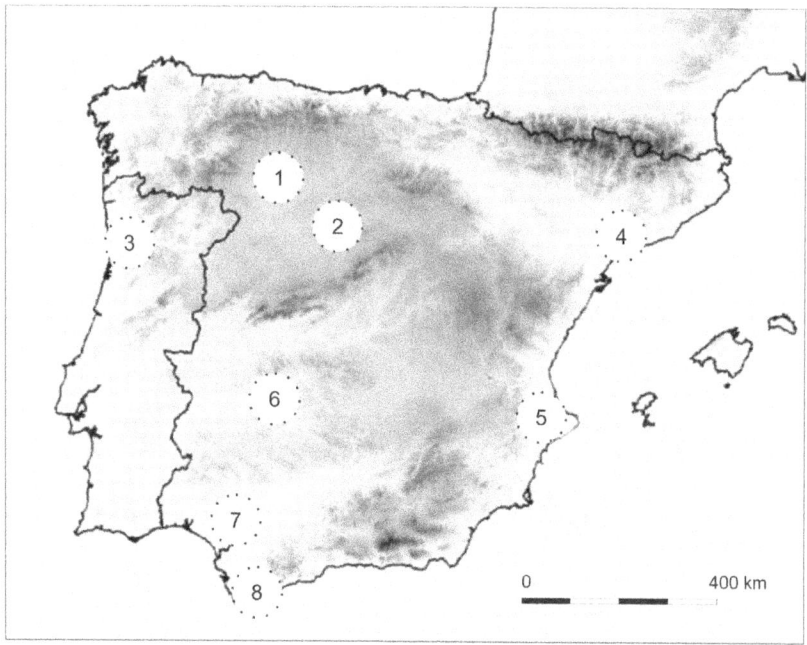

Figure 8 Map of the main territorial areas with landscape studies offering evidence of peasant occupation and production. (1) Sasamón (Burgos). (2) *Ager Salmantinus* (Salamanca). (3) *Bracara Augusta* (Portugal). (4) *Ager Tarraconensis* (Tarragona). (5) Alcoi Valley (Alacant). (6) Guadiana Valley (Badajoz). (7) Viar River Valley (Sevilla). (8) *Baelo Claudia* (Tarifa, Cádiz).

systematic prospecting of this same region (Frías 2010). An example would be El Mas d'Alfafar farm in the Alcoi Valley (Grau, Jimenez, and Sarabia 2021). The surveys carried out in this area identified a concentration of pottery between the 2nd century BC and the 2nd century AD within about 1000 m^2. The vast majority of ceramics consists of common Iberian and Roman types, basically large- and medium-sized containers, amphoras, and, to a lesser extent, tableware. Along with the common ware, pieces of terra sigillata-type tableware are also found, although in much smaller amounts.

This dense concentration of pottery probably provides evidence for a settlement from the early Roman period dating to the first quarter of the 1st century, as attested by test trenches. In fact, the excavations identified the façade of solid masonry built with large 60-cm-wide limestone blocks. This wall can be traced along a façade of more than 20 m, evidence of a rural building with solid walls two Roman feet wide (approx. 592 mm) and a tiled roof. The absence of luxury elements would indicate that we are looking at an early Roman farm and also corroborates that the surface vestiges correspond to that site.

At the settlement of Canèssia in the same region, an enclosure with a concentration of Roman pottery helped locate an ancient settlement of approximately 9000–10,000 m^2. To the south of the habitat, a strong concentration of ceramic roofing tiles and some human bones suggested a Roman necropolis associated with the settlement (Grau, Jimenez, and Sarabia 2021: 34).

Concentrations of finds, corresponding to the superficial archaeological signature we associate with these dispersed rural sites, are quite frequent in surveying and landscape studies. Thus, we can find them in a large part of the territories studied on the Iberian Peninsula, and a quick review indicates the ubiquity of these peasant farms.

Such sites are common in the *ager Tarraconensis* (the territory of the ancient Roman colony of *Tarraco*) on the Iberian Mediterranean coast. A total of 120 early Roman sites have been identified. Of them, 32 are classified as *villae* according to the materials found (e.g. mosaic floor remains); 29 are identified as rural establishments; and the remaining 53 are only labeled as pottery concentrations (Prevosti and Guitart 2011: 389). A little further north, in the interior of Catalonia in the Vallès region (Barcelona province) we find this same pattern. The settlement organized around the Congost road shows the coexistence of Roman *villae* along with a significant number of rural settlements that are interpreted as complex farms (Flórez and Palet 2012: 187–188, Figure 15). This northeastern region of Hispania perhaps has the greatest number of excavated farms, and they reveal an enormous range of structural types (Revilla 2022: 186–187, Figure 8).

The interior of the Iberian Peninsula offers a similar panorama. In the surveys of the *ager Salmantinus*, around modern Salamanca, indications of sites classified as *villae* have been detected along with a large number of sites that are difficult to assess; at least 22 archaeological sites have been recognized that make up a heterogeneous group including small rural sites (Ariño 2006: 319–329, Figure 3). The proximity of some of these sites suggests an association with small land plots.

Also in the interior of the Iberian Peninsula, in the Duero basin, the appearance in the early Roman era of small rural settlements is detected in an area where a dispersed settlement had not previously been documented. In this case, their low number would be a possible indicator of the gradual colonization of the land and perhaps the peripheral nature of this territory with respect to the main cities in the region (Tejerizo et al. 2015).

Continuing with examples from other areas, a case study from the western area of the Iberian Peninsula, in the territory of *Bracara Augusta* (Braga, Portugal), is also relevant to this project. These finds concentrations have once again been identified in that region. Evaluating their size or chronology is complex, although they are that type of small agricultural holding. The proximity of some *villae* to these dispersed nuclei would suggest dependence relationships with the larger centers. In addition to these dependent facilities, there would have been family-type agricultural exploitation units generally classified as farms (Carvalho 2007: 398–416).

Sometimes we find these farms grouped together to constitute village units where the communities would have consisted of various domestic groups or peasant families. The diversity of constructions inside these villages could point to functional or status differences between farmers with greater or lesser spending power, a diversity that would have been reflected in the habitats. However, within this variety of structures, no notable differences are identified that would allow us to recognize enclaves of a stately nature with luxurious residences and extensive agricultural processing facilities.

A good example from southern Iberia is found in the Viar River Valley, which has already been mentioned with reference to its excavated structures, but where the dispersion of surface finds suggests a concentration in the form of a village. The excavated structures and remains revealed by surveys show the appearance of various farms concentrated in an area of 7000m^2 (Fernández Flores and Carrasco Gómez 2013–2014). This would have constituted an agglomerated peasant community.

Also in southern Iberia, specifically in Tarifa (Cádiz province) in the territory of *Baelo Claudia*, surface surveys have revealed similar examples of diverse buildings grouped in spaces of around one or two hectares, sizes much larger than farms: for example, the Canchorrerillas 1 site (Grau, Jimenez, and Sarabia 2021). It emerged at the beginning of the 1st century, from which time it is possible to document a series of walls belonging to a minimum of four buildings, including a possible sheepfold and a granary. It covers a total area of 2.23 ha, in which both structures and surface finds are recorded. These would have been agricultural holdings that do not appear to have had luxury elements, given the absence of marble, stucco, or mosaic remains that would indicate the *pars urbana* typical of *villae*.

These settlements are also identified in other territories, and, judging by their size and remains, they can be considered village-type aggregates with an eminently peasant population. Also in this same category of grouped rural nuclei with a strong peasant component, we can link the secondary settlements of northwestern Iberia associated with *vici* or *castella* (farmsteads and small rural agglomerations).

In summary, practically all intensive surveys carried out in the territories of Hispania have provided superficial evidence of small archaeological sites that fall below the threshold to be considered as *villae*. A large part of these sites would have been farms and peasant settlements, as seen in the cases, in which excavations have been carried out. Thus, the panorama of the Hispania countryside is similar to that presented by other areas of the western central Mediterranean, like the one proposed by Kimberly Bowes on the distributed habitation model used to describe the settlement patterns of Roman peasants in Central Italy (Bowes 2020: 462–469). The persistence of such a dispersed settlement pattern could be interpreted as part of the tactics employed by these communities to increase the administrative costs of censuses and other state mechanisms related to taxation and the revenue acquisition of agricultural yields by Roman political authorities (Levi 1988: 71–94).

2.3 The Hidden Side of the Roman *villa*

At the beginning of this study, we indicated how the archaeological concept of *villa schiavistica* had eclipsed other more humble forms of Roman rural settlements. Beyond the historiographic issue, the truth is that in many cases this lack of visibility can be considered a stratigraphic phenomenon. The historiographic primacy given to the archaeological concept of *villa schiavistica* in the context of Spanish scholarship has meant in many cases that the remains of other phases recorded at these settlements have been obscured by the architectural and ornamental remains of the most monumental phases, even when they corresponded to a shorter chronological duration within the entire occupational sequence. For this reason, a taphonomic approach to the archaeological record of many *villae* can serve to reveal much more complex sequences than those normally reflected in the historical narratives traditionally linked to such sites in Roman Spain.

In some cases, we find that these monumental phases of Roman *villae* were superimposed over earlier settlements similar to the farms described

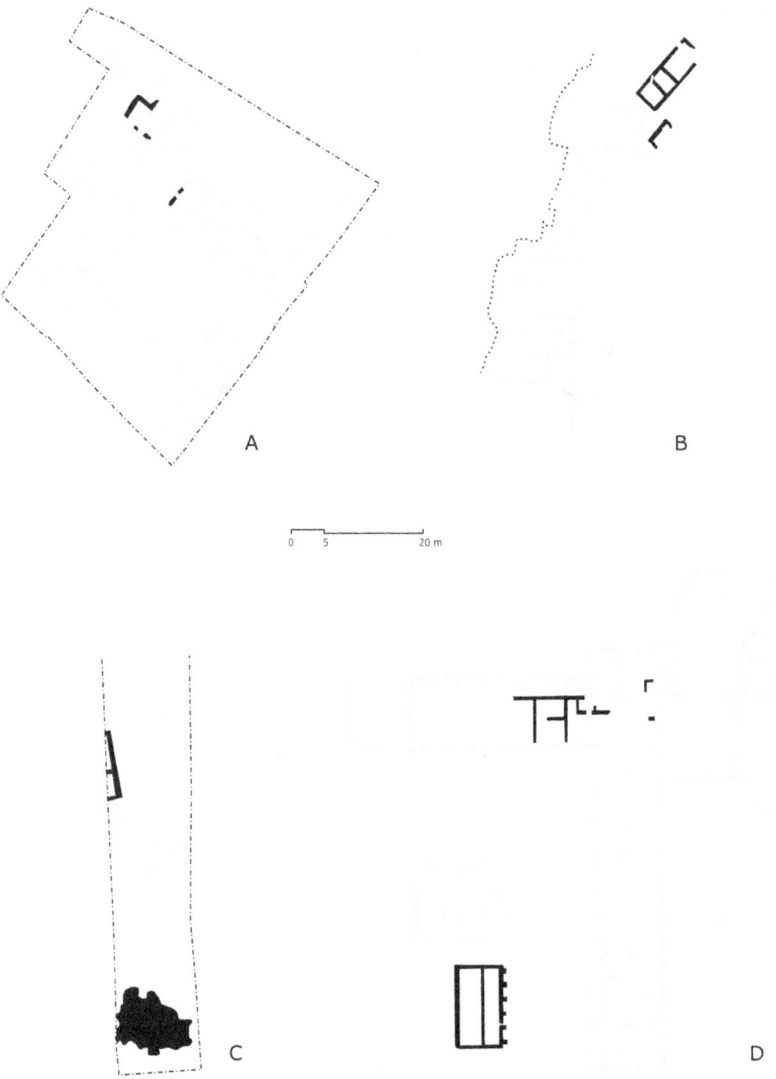

Figure 9 Plan of some Roman *villae* mentioned in text. (A) Los Cipreses (Jumilla), after Noguera Celdrán and Antolinos Marín (2009). (B) Les Planes de Roquís (Reus), after on Villaseca and Adiego (2000). (C) El Rasillo (Barajas), after Vigil-Escalera (2012). (D) Veranes (Asturias), after Fernández Ochoa, Gil Sendino and Orejas Saco del Valle (2004). In black: Structures corresponding to peasant settlements of the early Roman period. In grey: Structures corresponding to settlements of the late Roman period.

earlier. This is the case, for example, of the *villa* of Les Planes de Roquís (Reus) in the interior sector of the *ager Tarraconensis* (Figure 9: B). Here the structures of a subsequent early Roman rural settlement are superimposed on a small settlement of less than 20 m in length with three interior compartments that have an occupation horizon of between the late 2nd and the 1st century BC.

From the same late Republican period and also in the territory of the province of *Hispania Tarraconensis*, we find the remains of a first occupation phase of the *villa* of Los Cipreses (Jumilla, Murcia). The northern sector preserves the remains of walls corresponding to a small settlement that appears to be made up of at least three rooms (Noguera Celdrán and Antolinos Marín 2009: 194, Figures 3 and 5) (Figure 9: A).

In other sectors of Roman Spain, these "hidden" settlements are related to early Roman occupation phases discovered during systematic excavation of the residential part (*pars urbana*) of many *villae* monumentalized during the late Roman period. This is the case, for example, of the Roman *villa* of Almenara de Adaja-Puras (Valladolid), where various archaeological excavations carried out in the so-called Arroyuelo sector, about 150 m from the remains of the monumental *villa*, found several domestic structures occupied between the 1st and 2nd centuries AD. These structures consist of the remains of several dwellings built with rammed earth and vegetal cover, a hearth and a pit with clear remains of combustion. In addition to these housing structures, the excavation of a sector annexed to the remains of the monumental *villa* itself documented two silos cut directly into the bedrock (Sánchez Simón 2022).

In addition to the structural excavations, pollen recovery and analysis on columns and microdeposits in these sectors yield important evidence that confirms pasture and cereal farming as part of the productive activities carried out by the inhabitants of the first early Roman phase of the settlement. Finally, the analysis of the charcoal remains deposited in the aforementioned pit indicates its use to burn wood, which could perhaps be related to the exploitation of forestry resources to obtain resins.

Another occupation phase overshadowed by the remains of a late Roman *villa* is found at Veranes (Asturias) on the Cantabrian coast. Documented in that settlement, superimposed on the remains of several large rooms from the late Roman phase, were the remains of a structure that could have been part of a farm similar to those described earlier (Fernández Ochoa, Gil Sendino, and Orejas 2004) (Figure 9: D).

A similar case, this time located in the center of the Iberian Peninsula, is found at El Rasillo (Barajas, Madrid). The rescue excavations carried out here documented a complex settlement with various periods of occupation between the 1st and the 5th centuries AD (Bermejo Tirado 2017: 357). From a monumental point of view, most notable are the remains of a *villa* with a rectilinear ground plan and at least two rows of superimposed rooms that would have been built around the second third of the 4th century AD. It is with this phase that we have to associate the remains of a bathhouse previously recorded here. Prior to the construction of this monumental phase, however, the rescue excavations identified a small rural settlement with a rectangular shape, of which only the southwestern corner could be documented, and evidence of three rooms (Bermejo Tirado 2017: 357) (Figure 9: C).

Associated with the definitive abandonment of this settlement, the deposits that filled an adjacent pit were also excavated. It probably contained the abandonment remains of the last occupation phase of this peasant farm prior to the construction of the late Roman *villa*. The find contexts of this deposit, which are covered by the first leveling fills of the monumental *villa*, contained materials that allow us to establish a final chronology for this deposit situated around AD 325.

2.4 Squatters or Just Peasants? Late Antique Reoccupations of Roman *villae*

The remains of the monumental phases of the *villae* have not only obscured the evidence of preceding occupations; other later occupation phases have also been marginalized by current research. In many cases this concealment derives from taphonomic issues directly related to the formation of the archaeological record in the final phases of such settlements. In many cases, however, more than a methodological problem exists; it is a question of historiographic perspective. In this respect we can affirm that the archaeological analysis in recent decades of many of these late antiquity occupation phases documented in the Iberian Peninsula *villae* has been influenced by two fundamental historiographic models.

The first of these, fundamentally linked to classical archaeology, is that of the so-called squatters, which tends to conceive these late antique phenomena as illegal occupations (see Ellis 1988b: 572; López Palomo 2013–2014). This represents an exercise in presentism clearly influenced by conservative ideological concepts. Although this trend has generally been intrinsic to the emergence of the archaeological paradigm of the *villa schiavistica*, the truth is that critical voices have long been raised regarding such interpretation of the late antique archaeological record of the *villae* (Dodds 2019; Bermejo Tirado 2024).

The second historiographic narrative that today can be considered dominant in current scholarship is the so-called "end of the *villae*" (Chavarría 2007; Brogiolo and Chavarría 2008). This is a historiographic model developed by archaeologists specializing in the study of late antiquity, and it has caused a considerable dilemma in various recent studies of early medieval peasantry on the Iberian Peninsula. In short, it could be stated that this model could be considered as part of a general historical narrative emanating from an orthodox Marxist reading similar to that underlying the genesis of the archaeological concept of the *villa schiavistica*. This sees late antiquity as a period of transition between the slave and feudal modes of production (Francovich and Hodges 2003). As J. A. Quirós (2022) has pointed out, this historical narrative raises a series of fundamental problems. Perhaps the main one is the generalized linking of these levels of occupation to historical processes that are too abstract (e.g. the end of classical antiquity or the beginning of the Middle Ages) that do not take into account the different specific trajectories recorded in each settlement.

Next we compare some late antiquity occupations recorded in many of these *villae* with the aim of testing such narratives. We will focus on a more concrete discussion based on a more specific concept of the archaeological record in each case. Perhaps one of the best-known references for such late antiquity occupation is the *villa* of El Val (Alcalá de Henares). During its excavation the application – pioneering at the time – of a microspatial recording methodology made it possible to document in detail the vestiges associated with a structure of post holes located directly on the mosaic bed of one of the late Roman banquet rooms (*triclinia*) documented in the complex. The ground plan of this structure is similar to that of the wooden long-houses, one of the most common forms of domestic architecture in western Iberia during late antiquity (Tejerizo 2012).

The first excavation campaigns were less meticulous with regard to the microspatial record of this type of occupation phase in some sectors of the residential part (*pars urbana*) of the *villa* of Carranque (Toledo) (Patón Lorca 2001). As a result, it was impossible to document the traces of a similar reoccupation in this settlement in such detail. Despite this, it is possible to observe recesses and post holes in several sectors of the room decorated with the mosaic of Achilles and Briseis. As such, it is relatively easy to identify the remains of a hut base similar to that documented at the *villa* of El Val (Alcalá de Henares, Madrid).

A similar reoccupation has been described more recently at the *villa* of Horta da Torre (Fronteira, Alto Alentejo) (Carneiro 2020). Its detailed excavation attested a new occupation phase that began at an undetermined time in the 5th century AD. At that time, a large part of the various marble plaques that decorated the magnificent semicircular room (*stibadium*) was removed and reused to make a new level of paving, much more irregular and functional than the *opus sectile* of the late Roman phase (Carneiro 2020) (Figure 10). A longhouse structure was built on top of this with wooden posts similar to those mentioned at El Val and Carranque. The study of the finds linked to these occupation phases has allowed us to establish a chronology that could be taken to the second half of the 6th century AD (Carneiro 2020: 255). Another similar reoccupation phase, also related to a Roman *villa* in the southern quadrant of *Lusitania*, is that documented at Milreu (Teichner 2008).

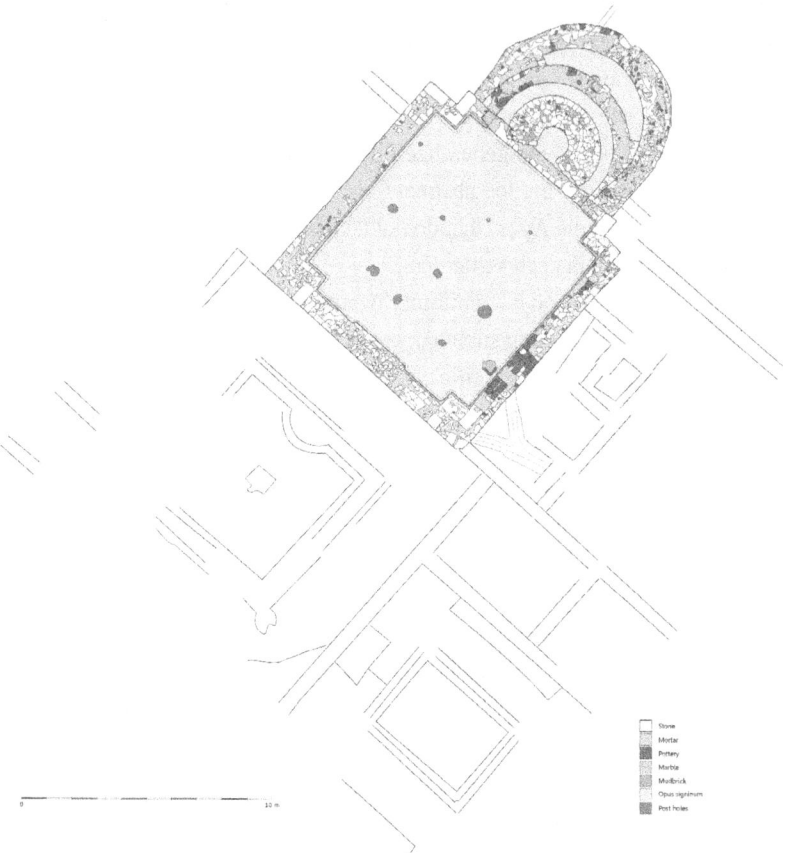

Figure 10 Plan of the *stibadium* sector of the Roman *villa* of Horta da Torre (Fronteira, Portugal), showing post holes excavated during the reoccupation in the late Antique period. (Image courtesy of Prof. André Carneiro, Universidade de Évora.)

Despite the undoubted parallelism of these examples, the analysis of the occupation sequences in other well-known Roman *villae* from the Iberian Peninsula illustrates diverse and specific trajectories, to which we refer. Perhaps one of the clearest examples is found in the *villa* of Torre de Palma, which is also relatively close to those of Milreu and (especially) Horta da Torre. At Torre de Palma it is not only possible to record a reoccupation of this kind in late antiquity, but, as the study of the construction sequence recorded in the settlement indicates, this same period can be considered the phase of greatest dynamism and monumentality of the settlement.

Another interesting case study for comparing differences in sequences is recorded in many *villae* at the already discussed site of Almenara de Adaja-Puras

(Valladolid). The sequence documented there includes some rustic structures that would have been part of a small baths facility, all date to between the 3rd and the first half of the 4th centuries AD. In the southern sector of this phase, the remains are of a small dwelling structure separated from the rest of the complex and surrounded by a series of large containers (*dolia*) buried in the ground (Sánchez Simón 2022). These vessels are interpreted as domestic pantry containers. Starch analyses carried out on several of these containers revealed that they were used to store wheat, barley, legumes, and acorns.

Built in the mid-4th century AD over the remains of this previous phase was the most monumental phase of the *villa* with its magnificent mosaics. At an early point in the 5th century, two rustic wings attached to this stately residence coincided with the final moments of the villa's occupation. Associated with this same phase is the construction of a small, isolated, square-shaped room about 5 m long. It contains a hearth composed of blocks with clear traces of fire abrasion. Among the abandonment deposits of this room are the remains of humble domestic furnishings that allow us to trace the occupation chronology of this small dwelling until well into the 5th century AD. Although all these structures were built when the stately residence was still in use, it is undeniable that their construction broke with the initial architectural module of the residential part (*pars urbana*) of the stately 4th-century-AD *villa*.

Finally, an occupation phase is documented at the site that is associated with the partial remains of a single structure with an elongated plan. It is a new housing core, the foundation of which overlaps the structures of the rustic wing attached to the southern part of the stately residence. This new settlement was built late in the 5th century AD, when the monumental residential sector (*pars urbana*) was already in disuse. Of this new building, only two walls of a room and a rammed earth floor are preserved. An important fact for the interpretation of all these late antiquity constructions is the coincidence in the use of the same rammed earth construction technique in the isolated room with a hearth, the rustic wings, and this last dwelling from the second half of the 5th century AD (Sánchez Simón 2022).

The example of Almenara de Adaja is especially relevant since it is one of the few Roman *villae* in the Duero valley that has been subjected to a systematic excavation applying stratigraphic criteria from the outset. Thanks to this we have been able to record a complex occupation sequence that can only be intuited in similar *villae* in the Alto Duero area.

Another example of a complex occupation sequence is found in the Roman villa of Fuente Álamo (Puente Genil, Córdoba). This Baetican *villa* is mainly known for the magnificent repertoire of mosaics that decorated the early Roman phase, as well as the stately residence probably built in the late 3rd century AD. The systematic excavations carried out by the team since 2005 have allowed the late antiquity reoccupation of several areas to be documented (Delgado and Jaén 2016, 2019).

Several rooms in the so-called Sector C of the *villa* were segmented with rammed earth walls to be reused as independent domestic structures (Figure 11).

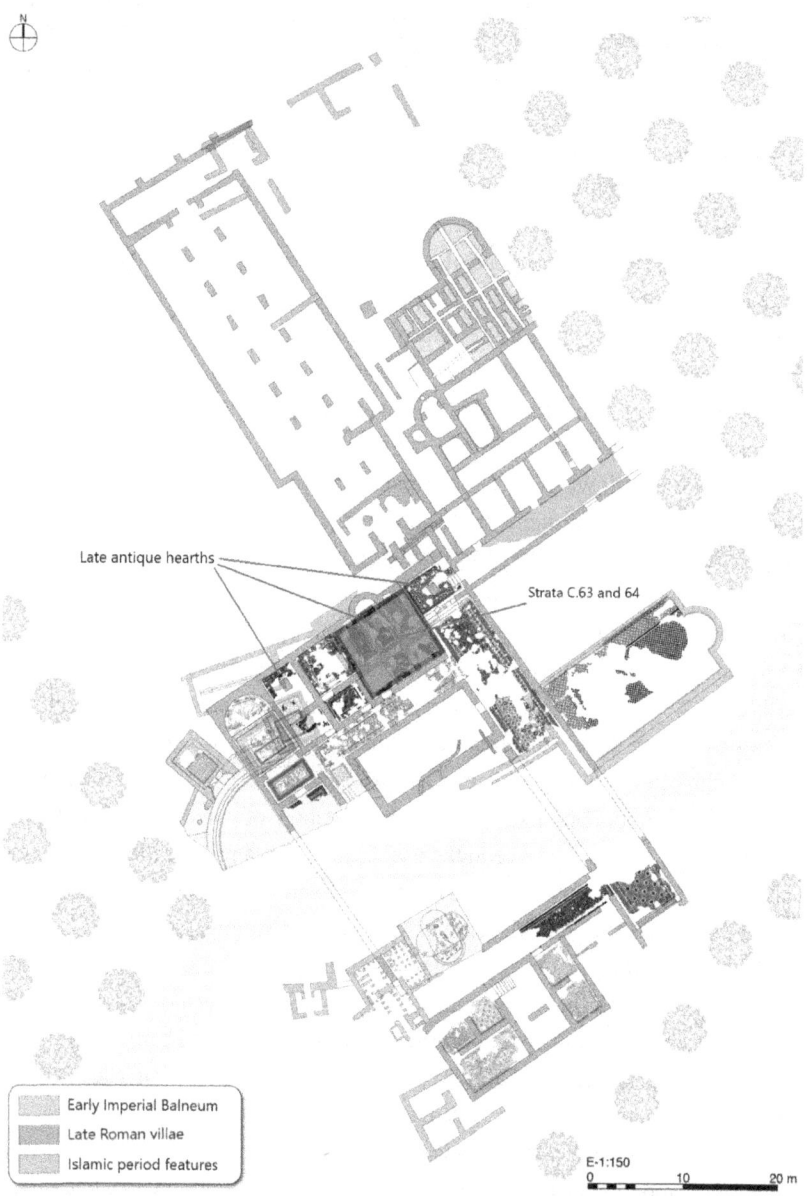

Figure 11 Plan of Sector C of the residential sector (*pars urbana*) of the Roman *villa* of Fuente Álamo (Puente Genil), showing renovations and the construction of hearths from the late antique phase. (Image courtesy of Manuel Delgado and David Jaén, Ayuntamiento de Puente Genil, Córdoba.)

This can be seen from the construction of a hearth made of ceramic blocks in each of the segmented rooms. Other elements of architectural decoration, such as a Corinthian-style capital, that adorned other sectors of the 4th-century-AD residential sector (*pars urbana*) were relocated to be used as part of the domestic furniture of these late antiquity residences.

In addition to these architectural features, the documentation of several closed deposits, previously to document abandonment, provided an opportunity to carry out a detailed study of finds associated with this late antiquity phase (see Bermejo, Moreno, and Colominas [2019: 258] for a chronological study). Importantly here, studying the domestic activities recorded here has allowed us to identify consumption patterns – with domestic tableware restricted in terms of the number of productions and morphological variables – and productive activities. The latter are related to a certain diversification with an orientation toward small-scale production undertaken in the domestic units that occupied these areas and coincide with what we could expect from a peasant-type economy (Bermejo, Moreno, and Colominas 2019: 263–271).

These and other examples of late antiquity reoccupations indicate that, even when there are no clear indications that architectural elements were removed and new structures replaced them, a detailed analysis of many abandonment deposits in monumental *villae* may document evidence for late antiquity occupation phases involving various groups or peasant communities (Bermejo Tirado 2024).

3 Roman Peasant Economy as Seen through Landscapes and Agrarian Systems

This section examines the correlation between agrarian labor within domestic units and the size of agricultural plots, shedding light on peasant landscapes in Roman Iberia. Work in the fields based on the labor available within the domestic unit – typical of peasant economies – would have had as a spatial correlate the small size of the plots of land compared to the model of large estates supported by paid or dependent labor typical of the *villa* model. Based on this postulate, the study of plots and agricultural land related to rural nuclei allows us to approach peasant landscapes.

The distribution by the Roman State of land plots shows the existence of smaller plots, indicating a tendency toward small-scale properties typical of peasant economies. Other archaeological evidence corroborates intensive agrarian production, as seen in surveys and geoarchaeological or micromorphological analysis. Examples across the Iberian Peninsula highlight intensive agricultural practices, including irrigation systems and terraced fields, that were aimed at maximizing productivity from small plots. This section underscores the intimate relationship between agrarian labor, plot size, and agricultural practices offering insights into the peasant landscapes of Roman Iberia.

3.1 Small Plots in *agri centuriati:* The Example of *Ilici*

The layout of small properties has been reflected in some historical data from the Roman period and especially in the exceptional document referring to the land distribution in the colony of *Iulia Ilici Augusta* (L'Alcúdia d'Elx, Alacant). The *sortitio* of *Ilici* is a bronze tablet that describes the distribution of the town's centuriation lands (Mayer and Olesti, 2001) (Figure 12). The allocation of plots is measured by the application of several Roman measurement units as the *porca* (210 m^2), *centuria* (approx. 50 ha), and the *iugera* (2518 m^2). The distribution attracted the attention of researchers due to the way it was allocated and the amount of land assigned to each *decuria* (approx. 5 ha), as the *centuria*

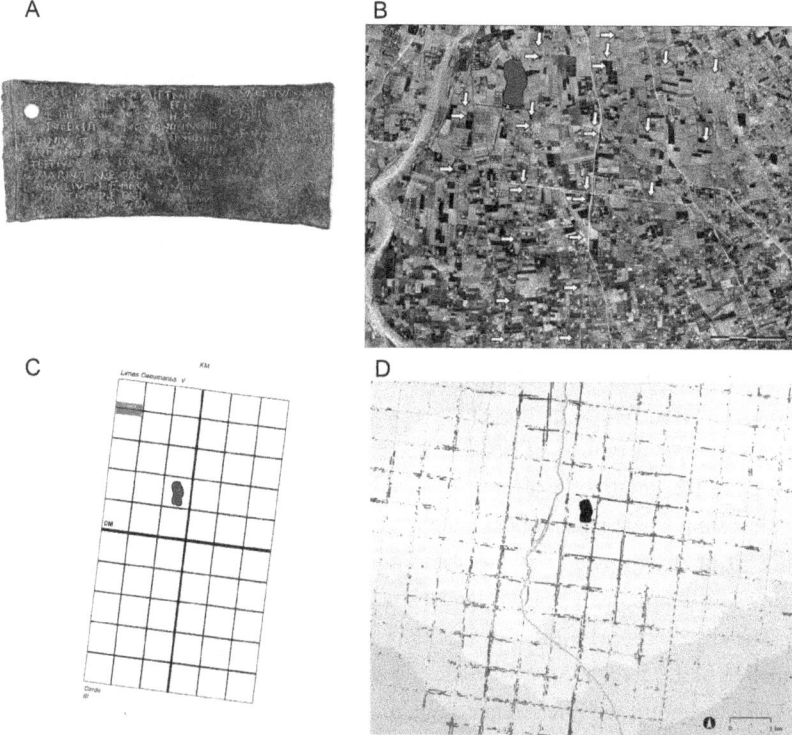

Figure 12 The centuriation of *Ilici*. (A) Bronze plaque with the *sortitio*. (B) Aerial photography of the 1956 American Flight with the location of the Roman town and the marks of the *pertica Ilicitana*. (C and D) scheme of the *pertica* (after Olesti et al. 2024).

did not easily adapt to other forms of division, such as the *modus triunviralis* that separates a *centuria* into four lots of 50 *iugera*. The specific method of land distribution in the *pertica Ilicitana* suggests a clear adaptation to small plots of land. Here we find smaller units with a distribution that is not so obvious, since each settler has 13 *iugera*, the equivalent of 3.2 ha, divided into two plots of 6.5 *iugera* corresponding to two different and adjoining *centuriae*.

This distribution is based on subdividing the *centuriae* into three parts, known as *trifinium* by surveyors, which normally gave rise to lots of 66 *iugera*. It followed the *conternatio* model described by Hyginus Gromaticus, which attributes one-third of a *centuria* to each colonist (Hyg. Grom. *De lim. const*, Th. 162, Mayer and Olesti 2002: 121). What we are interested in highlighting here is that in the case of *Ilici* each settler was granted a plot with a tenth of the land documented in other cases. To do this, each lot was distributed to a *decuria* and not individually to each settler. This particular aspect would indicate the concept of distribution of small plots and the generalization of small properties, as is typical of peasant farms. In reality, this is not a unique case, since there are mentions of similar cases, such as the territory of *Vibo Valentia* (Calabria, Italy), where 15 *iugera* were distributed to each of the *pedites*, or the proposals of the *rogatio Servilia* to distribute lots of 10 to 12 *iugera*.

The size plots assigned in the joint allocation of measured plots (*pertica Ilicitana*) presumably in places where water availability would have favored irrigation or intensive uses shows that this smaller size is linked to such agrarian management; ethnographic and historical data inform us of the uses and areas that each domestic unit would have worked. Thus, in traditional Mediterranean societies, the intensive peasant agrarian management usually consisted of family farm units of between 1 and 2 hectares (Halstead 1987: 84, Hodkinson 1988: 39), which fits well with these Roman plots.

3.2 Intensively Worked Plots in Other Farmlands: The Archaeological Evidence of Manuring

The archaeological signal for an intensive agrarian model can be seen in the surveying detection of pottery dispersed in what are known as *off-site* finds, that is, archaeological materials that are not directly associated either with places of residence or with the decomposition of primary archaeological deposits.

Intensive survey strategies have allowed us to recognize different distributions of archaeological finds that have left a distinct mark on the residential areas that are characterized by high densities and often associated with structures. In addition, low density of scatters have also been identified. Dispersed off-site pottery cannot be interpreted solely as the result of natural or anthropic post-depositional processes. Dispersion in areas surrounding high density points can be the result of ploughing or post-depositional effects on the supposed site. Beyond the closest areas, the intermittent and complex distribution pattern of the scatters invalidates the simple explanations of erosion and natural transportation processes. In some areas, detailed GIS-analysis of the dispersed scatters to test the manuring hypothesis has been carried out. These studies concluded that areas close to the potential sites were probably formed by the horizontal displacement of settlement debris; the movement of scatters was due to natural gravitational forces and to human removal of sediment in accordance with traditional rural practices, such as terracing or field modification. However, in areas further away dispersed scatters formed by domestic material including organic and inorganic debris leave the same observed ceramic signal in the surface both for the ancient scatters and for the debris related to premodern manuring (Grau Mira 2014: 128–129, Figure 7).

These features are most economically explained by the well-documented practice in historical and ethno-archaeological accounts of manuring from settlements into the cultivated landscape. The use of manure to improve the quality of soil is well attested in the textual references of the Roman agronomists. (A good description may be found in Poirier 2016: 280–282.) Cato (2nd century BC) described the tools used to spread the manure (*De Re Rustica*, V) and proposed that periods of bad weather should be dedicated to the cleaning of stables, barns, and all the buildings of the farm (*De Re Rustica*, XXXIX). Varro (1st century BC) mentioned the preferred location for a dunghill was near the farmstead (*Res Rusticae*, I, 38, 3). More detailed are the 1st-century-AD descriptions of manuring provided by Columella, who outlines the quantities needed for a certain area (*De Agricultura*, II, 5). In addition, he indicates that the farmer should collect all the waste from the farm, and keep it in a pit (*De Agricultura*, II, 14). Also Pliny the Elder (1st century AD) specified the soil that need improvement by manuring, the right time for fertilization, and the number of livestock needed to produce enough manure (*Naturalis Historia*, XVIII, 53). In sum, these references indicate well-established agrarian practices of using domestic waste for manuring the fields during Republican and Imperial times, between the 2nd century BC and 2nd century AD (Poirier 2016: 280–282).

Manuring has been a common practice in vineyards, orchards, irrigated fields, and other small plots in Iberia, as historical and ethno-archaeological studies demonstrate. These traditional practices were recorded in the 18th-century-descriptions of the agriculture in the Eastern regions of Spain. Ethno-archaeological studies of the pastoral landscapes in this area described the traditional manipulation of the manuring for the crops.

Overall, dispersed scatters of archaeological household waste suggest manuring and other farming practices, as has been proposed elsewhere in the ancient Mediterranean. This evidence of scattered pottery cannot be interpreted generally and uncritically, but must be discussed, in its local context. In this respect, our interpretation is that this superficial footprint of sherd carpets around sites of rural population reveals an intensive strategy that would have been based on crop rotation, irrigation and manuring, with household waste used to maintain the fertility of the fields. The mixed exploitation regime of crop growing and ovicaprine stockbreeding common to mid-mountain zones would have structured the productive scheme of these groups. Cross-cultural studies allow us to recognize these land uses as linked to small dwelling areas.

Examples of broad pottery sherd halos are found in various areas of the Iberian Peninsula, in which survey strategies based on the geolocation of all remains and the evaluation of the various densities have allowed them to be identified. In a recent field study in the Alcoi Valley (Alacant), the small areas of habitat in the Roman period associated with groups of peasant houses would have occupied between 0.8 and 1.1 ha, while the off-site record in the areas of intensive use – probably market gardens – next to the settlements, has allowed us to define perimeters of between 2 and 13 ha (Grau, Jimenez, and Sarabia 2021) (Figure 13: C).

In the interior of the Iberian Peninsula, we can point to other examples of this land use. For example, in the north of the Meseta, in the Odra and Brullés Valleys in the territory of *Segisamo*, systematic intensive prospecting has made it possible to recognize the dispersions of off-site materials that, once statistically processed, fit in well with the manuring hypothesis (García-Sánchez and Cisneros, 2013: 307) (Figure 13: B). In the Almar Valley (Salamanca province), after deploying an improved prospecting strategy, 11 percent of the enclaves originally catalogued as archaeological sites in the Archaeological Inventory are now seen to correspond to the category of off-site finds (Ariño and Soto 2016: 51), which would suggest intensive agricultural uses. Also related to intensive uses, a system of terraced fields with abundant off-site material has been located in the *Calagurris* area of the Ebro Valley (Zaragoza province). It is linked to a plot of land equipped with an irrigation system (Ariño 2003: 110).

A final example takes us to the Roman territories of southwestern Iberia, specifically the Guadiana Valley (Mayoral et al. 2014). Intensive surveys carried out in this area have yielded the same surface signatures related to early Roman settlements identified by concentrations of finds and other dispersions related to intensive production spaces (Mayoral et al. 2014: 1410, Figure 10) (Figure 13: A).

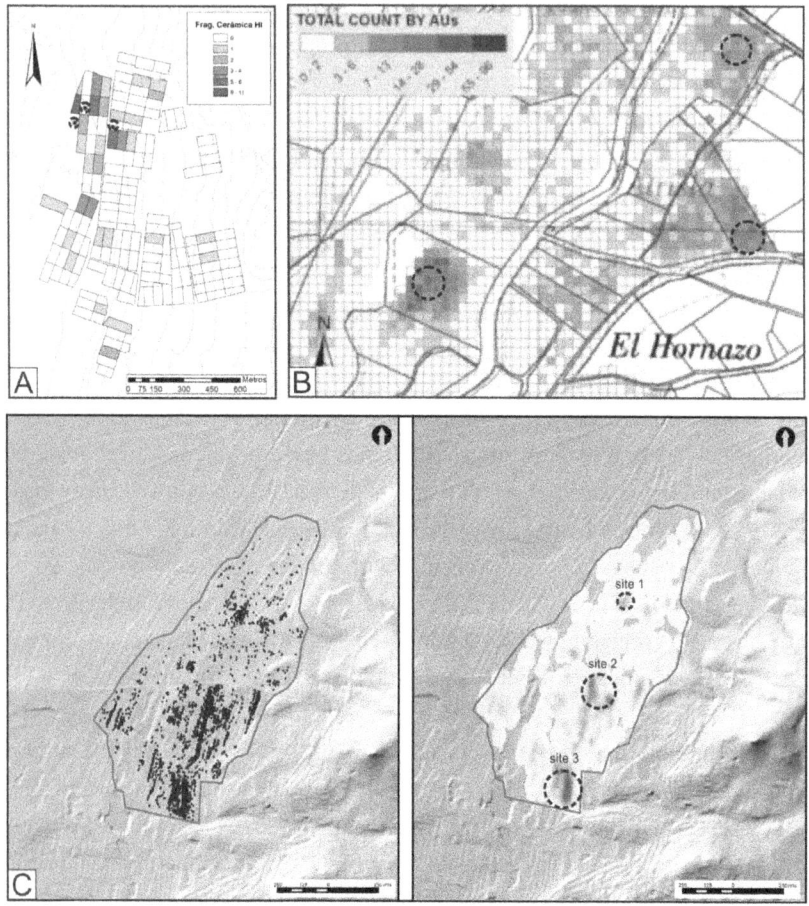

Figure 13 Survey areas in various regions of Roman Iberia, indicating the location of farmsteads, areas of dense material concentration, and halos of ceramic dispersals associated with manuring. (A) Guadiana Valley (Badajoz); (B) Sasamón (Burgos); (C) Banyeres de Mariola (Alacant).

3.3 Terracing, Irrigation, and Landscape Signatures

Finally, we would like to point out the existence of agricultural terraces, linked to rural settlements, built to improve and increase the agricultural production of small plots. Such evidence is elusive and has barely been documented in archaeological studies. Only with the development of large-scale archaeological interventions related to high-impact public works has it been possible to describe them.

Studies of terraced landscapes have been developed in various hilly regions of Iberia. Some good examples in the mountainous area of the North-western regions of the province of *Lusitania,* in the areas of Sierra de Francia (Salamanca) and in neighboring *Hispania Citerior* at Pino del Oro (Zamora) (Ruiz del Árbol 2006; Sánchez-Palencia and Currás 2021). These ancient terraces are especially frequent in the area of eastern Iberia where during the same period as that of our study, that is, between the 2nd centuries BC and 2nd century AD, they have been identified at La Foia de Manuel, El Ramblar and La Vila Joiosa. All of them are similar and are characterized by modifying gentle slopes, always with slopes of less than 6 degrees of inclination, located in alluvial fans and with soils of average thickness of around 1–1.5 m. These are generally small plots that have been modified to improve growing conditions, especially for moisture retention.

A recent study based on a multi-proxy archaeological approach permitted the study of traces of agricultural uses in constructed terraces dated to the Roman period in Banyeres de Mariola (Alacant) (Grau et al. 2023, 2024). The micromorphological, geochemical, and bioarchaeological features allowed us to study Roman agricultural use (Figure 14). Next, we will focus on the analysis of the features, as a good case study that allowed us to characterize a specific agrarian strategy and propose a framework for its socioeconomic functioning.

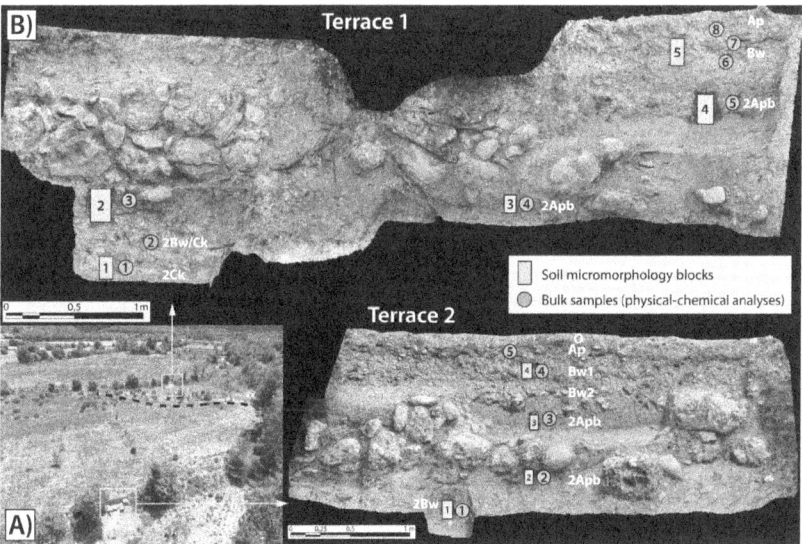

Figure 14 (A) Image of the Roman terraces of Banyeres de Mariola (Alacant). (B) Profile of excavated terraces with the soil sequence in relation to the constructed terraces and the simples obtained. Terrace 1: Ah & Bw: Modern-Medieval Period; 2Apb: Roman terraced Field; 2Bw/Ck & 2Ck: Ground base. Terrace 2: Ap, Bw1& Bw2: Modern-Medieval Period; 2Apb: Roman terraced field; 2Bw: Ground base.

The first aspect we would like to highlight is the small scale of the projects involving the construction and maintenance of plots of terraces and the continuous work and use, covering a surface of around 6 ha. Peasant households mobilized labor for the configuration and maintenance of these crop fields. Labor management is precisely one of the keys to defining this agrarian strategy, as opposed to other more widespread models based on *villae* systems and the tilling of extensive dry land, the other proposals for Roman agriculture in Iberia (Ariño and Chávez 2019). We can distinguish different phases in the construction and management of this terraced peasant landscape:

Plot construction. Land use began with the leveling of the natural terrain. The terrace retaining walls were built with blocks of local limestone of highly variable sizes, in which large blocks (of more than 110 cm) were interspersed with small stones (of approximately 30 cm). Subsequently, the soil was thickened by adding domestic waste, including organic contributions (ashes and detritus) and pottery sherds.

One of the purposes of the construction of terraces could have been the cultivation of species with deep roots, such as the vine detected in the palynological records, as we will describe later. However, the palaeobotanical evidence indicates that the most frequent crops were cereals, the roots of which do not require deep layers, although the greater soil thickness would have improved the yields.

The leveling of the slope into horizontal plots would also have facilitated water retention and irrigation, traces of which have been detected in the geochemical composition, as alkaline pH, probably from carbonates, would also have been the result of prolonged irrigation and evapotranspiration processes. It is worth highlighting micromorphological data pointing to a humid local environment as shown by the presence of needle fiber calcite, which is produced by fungal biomineralization in vadose environments.

Field tillage and maintenance. The terraces were subjected to constant ploughing to maintain the field fertility through tillage, irrigation, and continuous manuring. Micromorphological evidence and physicochemical results indicate the presence of buried cultivated horizons, with textural pedofeatures such as dusty clay coatings, sedimentary crusts, disaggregated microstructure, and other features related to colluvium, suggesting the use of agricultural implements on bare soil surfaces.

Regarding soil fertilization, to the aforementioned contributions of water, we have to add the geochemical composition of the soil, with trace elements related to fertilization. Ca, P, and Sr concentrations may be associated with the presence of bone remains, elements such as Ba and Mn with humus, while K has been associated with ash and charcoal, and Cu is also related to ash, fires and waste.

In general, all these components blend in well with the organic contributions from the domestic waste that would have accompanied the ancient pottery. This coarse fraction is not only a clear testimony of the domestic contribution and chronological affiliation, but would also have improved the texture of agricultural soils thanks to an increase in porosity that would have facilitated the development of microbiota.

Crops and cultivation. The results of the pollen records of these Roman fields indicate cereal and vinegrapes cultivation was also identified. The phytolith assemblages were dominated by *Pooideae* grasses, which includes major cereals such as wheat (*Triticum* sp.) and barley (*Hordeum* sp.), which are consistent with dominated pollen *Cerealia*. It is therefore possible that vines and cereals were cultivated at the same time on the Roman terraces. The crops grown on it – mainly cereals – appear to be suitable for the generation of surpluses, but in reality may have served the subsistence needs of the peasant groups.

3.4 Intensification: A Peasant Strategy

The identification and analysis of agricultural intensification based on settlement patterns and agricultural practices open up the possibility of recognizing peasant forms of socioeconomic organization. Intensification may include innovations and the investment of working capital in constructions that leave a permanent mark in the archaeological record and may therefore be recognized in the surface surveys. Some innovations create landesque capital that, once formed, persists with the sole need for maintenance of infrastructures (Brookfield 1984: 16). Examples of this are cultivation terraces or irrigation canals. Other procedures require continuous application, and their permanent footprint on the ground is the sum of intensive practices (Brookfield 1972: 32). These practices would have developed over more or less prolonged periods of time, and include manuring, the main footprint detected in our case study.

We owe one of the main theories on intensification to Boserup (1965, 1981), who argued that population growth would have led to demographic pressure on resources and a need for agricultural intensification. These growing populations with limited access to land would have encouraged the adoption of new agricultural strategies or technologies. In this context, farmers reduced fallow and maximized land use or developed agro-engineering works. In the case of the Roman peasantry however, it is unlikely that population growth was the driving force behind intensification, as the geographical space with large empty areas of cultivation would appear to rule out demographic saturation.

In addition to population growth, other researchers have proposed that other variables played a key role in intensification and frequently have been attributed to social demands, such as tributary extraction related to political economy, and the role of trade in intensive agricultural systems (Brookfield 1972: 36–38). Some initiatives and investments were possibly related to large dominial estates or to the intervention of the Roman state.

In our opinion, however, the determining vector in intensification would be the socioeconomic organization of agricultural work based on the household and its labor force along the lines proposed in the smallholders model of Netting. This researcher emphasized the role of the small household group – the nuclear or polygynous family – as the social unit that normally mobilized labor, organized consumption, and exercised ownership over a small group of intensively farmed plots of land (Netting 1993: 13). It is possible that the predominant role was played by the initiatives of small peasant groups without strict dependence on external factors. Although they were groups with connections to neighboring regions through political relations and exchange networks, their economic activity was oriented toward satisfying the group's own needs and its perpetuation on the land based on continuous investment.

4 Roman Peasant Networks and Economic Hubs

This section discusses specialized production, trade, markets, and commerce in rural landscapes, suggesting the existence of decentralized networks that complemented urban markets. Ways of integrating peasant economies into Roman distribution networks are proposed as a means to concentrate and channel resources. Peasant settlements are not isolated, disconnected entities. On the contrary, they form networks of nuclei structured around rural districts, *pagus* and *vici*, the organizational framework of Roman rural communities. Recent studies have shown that practically all the epigraphic references to *vici* and *pagi* are from Roman administrative structures that managed rural districts and that they were developed subsequent to conquest and implantation processes that do not respond to situations prior to the arrival of Rome (Tarpin 2002: 144).

As studies of the *vici* and *pagi* of the central-southern Italic world have shown, they were not pre-Roman entities that survived, but rather territorial structures that were resignified under the new Roman organization to accommodate peasant communities in non-urban areas (Stek 2009). This administrative situation allows us to identify not only the existence of these rural communities, but also their own social and economic organizational forms.

4.1 Trade and Commerce in Rural Landscapes

In general, research into Roman commerce and trade has prioritized mercantile networks organized around towns and systems oriented toward interregional exchange within the framework of the imperial economy. This assumes the role of the local territory structuring markets, to which resources from the area would be drawn. These structures are based on the geographical thinking of the center-periphery models of Von Thünnen and Christaller and are fomented in scholarship by the urban-centric emphasis of classical archaeology. In this state of affairs, the possibility of recognizing other forms of integration and analysis of settlement networks with smaller scales of interaction and less archaeological visibility have barely been explored. However, these spatial schemes were not necessarily mutually exclusive, since rural settlements could well have organized other decentralized networks (Knitter and Nakoinz 2018) structured by non-urban settlements that would have functioned as system nodes.

The connections that linked rural groups could have been established through various forms of management and administration. For example, previous research has proposed that there were exchange structures that complemented the urban market systems (De Ligt 1993). Thus, fairs would have been held on the occasion of religious festivities, rural markets (*nundinae*), or stately markets (*domanial* markets) (De Ligt 1993: 155–198). These models may be of interest for the interpretation of territorial schemes and the archaeological evidence that show features in accordance with these interpretative lines.

On the one hand, in various rural areas the largest settlements of the system – *villa*-type nuclei – would have been the centers of estates (*fundi*), around which the peasant settlements would have orbited. These larger centers present functional and productive structures, including rows of storehouses and processing facilities that would have allowed the production of peasant farms to be concentrated for circulation on a regional scale. In these microregions, small-scale peasant production was oriented neither toward mere subsistence production nor toward maximizing production for exchange, but rather somewhere in between where some surpluses would have been generated. The concentration of these surplus productions from peasant domestic units could have been channeled toward urban markets.

It is difficult to document spaces in *villae* dedicated to the celebration of weekly markets or *nundinae*. In the Iberian Peninsula we have the example of the Roman villa of Valdetorres del Jarama, where hypothetically one of these markets was held in a polygonal building dependent on a *villa* (Brogiolo and Chavarria 2008: 30). In turn, these meetings could be taken advantage of by the owners of some *villae*, since the celebration of these exchanges in their domains could offer them the possibility of economic control over the dependent groups, as has been observed in several *villae* in North Africa (Chaouali 2002).

Following this scheme, the overlords of the countryside would not have obtained extensive economic benefits, given the mediocre levels of wealth these towns usually show; however, in exchange they would have been able to exercise clear social dominance over the peasant populations. These centers stand as connectors with the outside world, facilitating the linking of peasant economies with urban and interregional trade networks.

4.2 Peasant Networks

Historians of the Roman market economy have focused their attention on the archaeological record linked fundamentally to the trade of imported goods, such as *amphorae* and tableware, at macro-level and interregional scales. Less attention has been paid to other scales of trade, such as local or peasant networks. Recently, a new line of studies concerning the economic integration of peasant sites through network analysis and quantitative study of systematic household archaeology data from peasant settlements has been developed. Such studies have been carried out in the central region of Iberia (Moreno, Brughmans, and Bermejo 2023).

The patterns inferred from the application of network analysis suggest a series of implications for the interpretation of the economic structure of these peasant sites. A certain degree of integration in trade networks of peasant sites is clearly demonstrated. Peasant sites were exposed to imported goods, these nonlocal goods show comparable distribution patterns to local goods, and many peasant sites have many artifacts of all provenance scales in common. Yet, most site assemblages are distinct. The subtle patterns of economic interaction shown in these networks cannot be associated with models of strong integration used by some part of recent scholarship to characterize the Roman market economy (Temin 2013; Brughmans and Poblome 2016). This weak integration is especially reflected by the scarce evidence for interprovincial connections in this region of inland Iberia (Moreno, Brughmans, and Bermejo 2023).

In contrast to the generalizing view of the formalist and sustantivist models, the results show complexity and diversity among the economic profiles documented at settlement level. The network approach therefore offers a quantified, but nuanced, exploration of specified relational markers of economic integration; it has the potential to identify the degree of the presence of these markers and to place Roman provincial peasant sites along a spectrum of economic integration.

4.3 Rural Worship Sites and Their Role in Place-making

A final aspect that deserves to be highlighted is the economic potential to promote trade that can be attributed to the places of worship. The association between places of cult and rural markets is widely attested in antiquity. It is basically favored by two aspects inherent to these sacred spaces: as a meeting place and being under divine protection that would guarantee trust in the transactions conducted. The series of objects deposited at the sanctuary, including tableware, lamps, and coins, is a good example of availability of imported goods directly related to trade.

Research on the Italian countryside has shown that the rural district (*pagus*) acquired an important role in the territorial administration with diverse functions. These included religion, for which its own places of worship were provided, according to some ancient sources. For example, Siculus Flaccus (*de Condicionibus Agrorum* 14-15) mentions *sacra diversa*, referring to the diversity of cults practiced in the rural districts (*pagi*). In fact, the religious dimension has been interpreted as a fundamental aspect for the definition and creation of new communities and the reorganization of the territory and peasant groups (Stek 2009: 171). Following this example, we would like to focus our attention on the role of the rural sanctuaries of Iberia as nodes that structured these peasant networks.

Many places of worship were spread across the rural districts of Hispania and only recently have they begun to attract attention as social centers and places of peasant identity (Sinner and Revilla 2022). The purpose of these studies is to understand religious behaviors in the socioeconomic and political circumstances of a rural environment. In other words, to approach the often elusive world of Roman peasant ideology.

The material culture offers us the key to unlocking peasant agency, since in most cases these are places of worship with simple offerings of a repetitive nature, generally items of tableware, lamps, or coins. The standardization of votive offerings reflects the fact that no obvious social competition was signaled by costly offerings, as are typical of the ritual dynamics among the elites of urban environments, where exist expensive gifts, dedications of inscribed monuments, or the erection of constructed elements. This does not mean that differences in status and position were not expressed through items that are not visible in the archaeological record, such as perishable products offered or consumed. Neither can we assume that everyone had access to the imported tableware and other objects deposited. Without a doubt the homogeneity of the objects signifies equity in the votive deposits. These simple objects inhibited the display of personal wealth and ostentation. This is typical of peasant groups when compared to those contexts, in which donations involved an enormous use of economic resources.

Certain religious celebrations typical of rural areas would have been held in these sanctuaries. They would have included the *Sementivae* or *Lustrationes*

Pagi and, specifically, the *Paganalia* (Stek 2009: 173–177), with cults that formed part of a structure with deep agrarian roots. The main description of the *Paganalia* is provided by Dionysius of Halicarnassus in his *Roman Antiquities* (4.14-15). His detailed analysis has served as the basis for the formulation of the administrative role that underlies this religious festival (Stek 2009: 174). Dionysius (4.15) points out how the *Paganalia* festivities fostered community identity and facilitated the census of the rural population through three actions.

Firstly, a community meeting took place (σύνοδον; 4.15.4), which indicates that it was held in a place common to several settlements and that it favored community-building through ritual aggregation in the shared space. Secondly, there was the payment of coins (νόμισμα; 4.15.4) that were used to count the population that attended the festival and, therefore, had the effect of a census. Each participant, whether man, woman, or child, offered a different coin. In this way, the person presiding over the celebrations established the census by age and gender groups. Tarpin (2002) suggests that the rural census organized in districts (*pagi*), at least judging from Dionysius' description, appears to have been primarily aimed at taxation.

The coins, therefore, allowed a census function to be attributed to these places of worship and in that respect their frequent discovery in places of worship can be related, in addition to their own meanings as offerings. A quick review of the sanctuaries on the Mediterranean fringe of Hispania clearly reflects this material reality (Grau, Amorós López, and Segura 2017: 194–198). We see this in the sanctuary of La Cueva Negra de Fortuna (Murcia province), which is set in an extraordinary baths complex in use from the early 1st to the 17th centuries AD. This consists of three Roman-Republican examples, the state of conservation of which prevents us from refining their chronology. Corresponding to the 1st to the 2nd centuries AD is a collection of 41 coins that has been interpreted as having been thrown into the spring as offerings to the tutelary divinities of the place. Other examples demonstrate these same practices, and, although the number of coins is small, they undoubtedly represent a minimal portion of those used in antiquity. In La Serreta de Alcoi (Alacant province) we find a deposit of 46 coins perfectly framed between the 3rd and the late 4th centuries AD. At Cova de les Meravelles a collection of 39 coins dating from the 2nd century BC and the 4th century AD was recovered, some in poor condition. In Santa Bàrbara (Castelló) an interesting collection of coins was discovered made up of 86 specimens from various periods. In the nearby sanctuary of L'Alt de Pipa, reference is also made to the probable discovery of some coins, which hinders any assessment of their significance and impact in that place.

In summary, sanctuaries and cult places allow us to recognize specific peasant community practices and also to approach the cultural values and religious beliefs that contributed to forming the group's identity. A Roman rural sanctuary, therefore, allows us to understand the way in which the subaltern classes and peasant groups were able to build a religious environment, in which to recognize their place in the world. In other words, to construct a religious landscape appropriate to their needs and their perceptions of space and place.

5 Peasant Economies and Roman Markets

The complementarity of peasant economies and interprovincial markets is explored here within the framework of the imperial economy. We look at patterns of household commodity consumption derived from regional markets and thus requiring household surplus production for trade (Figure 15). Finally, we shall examine the role of peasant wine production in the large producing and distributing areas of the Mediterranean coast.

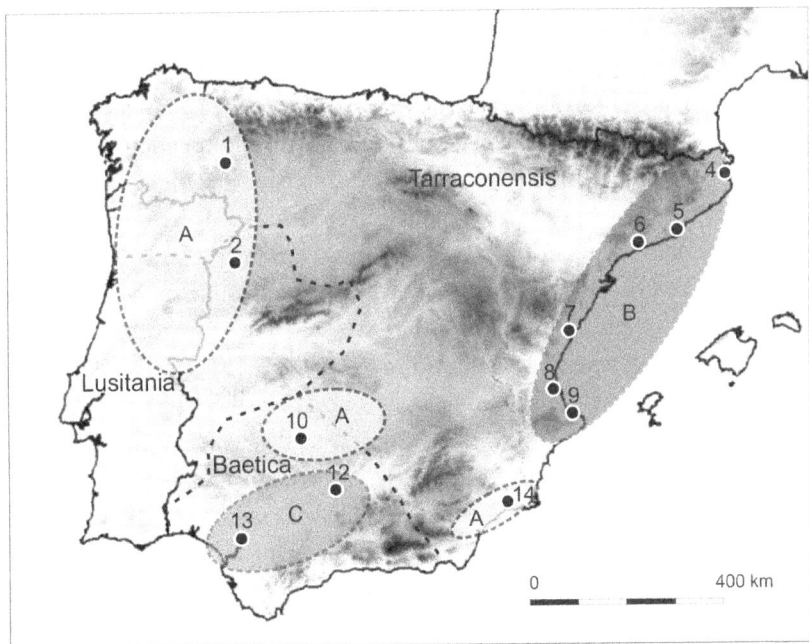

Figure 15 Map of areas with specialized economies involving peasant production: (A) Mining zones. (B) Viticulture in the *Tarraconensis*. (C) Olive cultivation in the *Baetica*.

5.1 The Role of Peasantry in Commercial Agrarian Economies: The Eastern and Southern Iberia

The Mediterranean edge of the Iberian Peninsula, characterized by an abundance of flat, fertile land, underwent a profound landscape transformation during the Roman period. Changes were designed to bring about a major increase in wine production to meet the demands of interprovincial markets (Remesal, Revilla, and Martí Oliveras 2019). Excavations have documented wine-production facilities (*torcularia*) associated with many of these settlements, including several presses and pools for the collection of must. The discovery of many such installations all along the littoral of *Hispania Citerior* has served to reveal the degree of technological development linked to the intensification of wine production during the Roman period.

An essential factor in understanding the configuration of agrarian landscapes in these coastal territories is their integration into interprovincial trade circuits. In addition to their role as organizing centers for the rural territories of these sectors of the Iberian Peninsula, Roman colonies and municipalities such as *Emporiae* (Empúries, Girona), *Barcino* (Barcelona), *Tarraco* (Tarragona), *Saguntum* (Sagunt, València), *Valentia* (València), and *Dianium* (Dènia, Alacant), among others, were efficient commercial ports that facilitated the export of a large part of the regional wine production. Archaeology has given us a detailed insight into the development of these trade networks. The quantitative study of amphorae production in these sectors of *Hispania Tarraconensis* – primarily Laietanian amphorae during the late Republican period and locally produced Dressel 2–4 amphorae during the early Imperial period – has revealed the historical evolution of these exports (Járrega and Berni 2016).

An important factor in the wine economy was the restructuring of rural settlement patterns. In these regions, it has been possible to document the establishment of rural sites that can be ascribed to the classical *villa* model based on slave or dependent labor. However, not all rural settlements in these sectors can be related. Data from various survey projects, already quoted, undertaken both in the *ager Tarraconensis* and in other southern coastal sectors as the *ager Dianiensis* reveal an increase in the number and variety of rural settlements during the early Imperial period, mostly small sites. This evidence has also been used to propose demographic growth in these sectors of the province (Sinner and Carreras 2019) mostly linked to peasants and small and medium-sized landowners.

In the case of Southern Iberia, in the province of *Baetica*, an even more profound reconfiguration took place under the direct supervision of the Roman administration. A large part of the Baetican countryside was destined for olive oil production under Roman state control. As a result, most of the region was integrated into the army supply (*annona*) system imposed by the new Roman imperial administration (Remesal, Revilla, and Martí Oliveras 2019), which was intended to supply the huge demand for agricultural products generated by the *Urbs*, as well as by the troops stationed on the northern border (*limes*) of the Empire.

Although no systematic intensive surveys exist for large parts of *Baetica*, several authors (Ponsich 1998) suggest that much of its land was parceled out using a medium-sized module that some Roman *agrimensores* defined technically as a *latus fundus* (equivalent to a *quinarius*, a quarter of a normal centuriation plot, which amounted to 25 *centuriae* of 200 *iugera* each, so around 50 ha). However, no traces of such centuriated land have been preserved that would allow us to affirm the generalized presence of these large states (*latifundia*) in the countryside of *Baetica* during the early Imperial period. On the contrary, scholars such as J. Remesal (2016) suggest that the ownership structure prevalent in these territories, dedicated to olive oil production, was a landscape of smallholdings, based on a module that Columella, who was born in the region at *Gades*, knew as the *porca*, a module of 30 x 130 Roman feet that originated in *Baetica*; that is, small plots of less than an *iugerum*, or 2500 sq. m. All this, together with the dense urban network established in the Guadalquivir Valley between *Hispalis* (Sevilla) and *Corduba* (Córdoba), where the Roman towns (*municipia*) are spaced close to one another, suggests that, at least in the places closest to the cities, these olive oil–producing landscapes were in the hands of small and medium-sized landowners during the early Imperial period.

5.2 The Contribution of Peasantry in Mining Economies: Northwestern Iberia

As Roman domination took hold of the mountainous regions of the northwest, the exploitation of the gold-bearing areas, some of the most important of the Empire, developed and became one of the priorities of the Roman authorities. An extraordinary example is Las Médulas (León), a vast gold-mining area exploited under the so-called mountain collapse (*ruina montium*) system described in a well-known passage by Pliny the Elder (Orejas and Sánchez Palencia 2002), which has left a profound mark on the landscape. Archaeologists have documented hundreds of channels at this site that were used to accumulate large volumes of water that were then released suddenly to cause the mountainside to collapse. Subsequently, the resulting sediment was filtered to extract the gold. The Roman method of gold mining involved altering the landscape on an unprecedented scale.

We highlight now how a distinctive peasant settlement system developed, linked to mass-scale mining, requiring substantial food supplies for mine laborers. In addition to the hydraulic infrastructure and the remains of landslides resulting from the accumulation of mining sediment, it has been possible to locate agricultural areas in the mountains with terraces showing that crops were grown to supply the area's populations. This is also the case in relation to the mining operations in the Sierra de Francia (Salamanca province) in *Lusitania* (Ruiz del Árbol 2005). At Las Cavenes (El Cabaco, Salamanca), digital modeling created with LIDAR has revealed a large area of agricultural terraces linked to the Roman peasant settlement of Fuente de la Mora, occupied from the 1st to the 3rd centuries AD. This high-altitude agricultural area would have been devoted to intensive exploitation of the soil based on models of horticulture and chestnut-tree cultivation designed to make the communities working in the mining areas self-sufficient (Sánchez-Palencia and Currás 2021).

In sum, intensification of peasant economies appears to have been crucial in two key aspects: peasant communities served to maintain the workforce in large-scale mining operations in northern Spain and Portugal; and the increase of agrarian activity was related to the needs of alimentary supplies of growing populations of miners and laborers.

6 Conclusions and Future Directions

We now synthesize the main points from the previous sections and the economic implications they entail. It is important to move away from a historicist view of the Mediterranean past that associates the slave mode of production with the ancient world and the beginning of the peasant mode of production with the early medieval world (Francovich and Hodges 2003; Bowes and Gutteridge 2005; Wickham 2005; Chavarría Arnau 2007; Diarte-Blasco 2018; Quirós Castillo 2022). Finally, we outline analytical lines and key concepts that will guide other future projects analyzing peasant economies in the Roman period in the Iberian Peninsula and beyond.

Our Element volume challenges the traditional view of Roman agrarian production based on large slave-managed estates, the so-called *villae*. It aims to redefine the role of peasant communities in Roman Iberia by examining archaeological evidence and adopting an anthropological approach (Figure 16). Key objectives include identifying archaeological proxies for peasant communities and redefining their economic structures within the broader context of Roman economic history. We shall outline here the directions now open for future research on rural Roman economies.

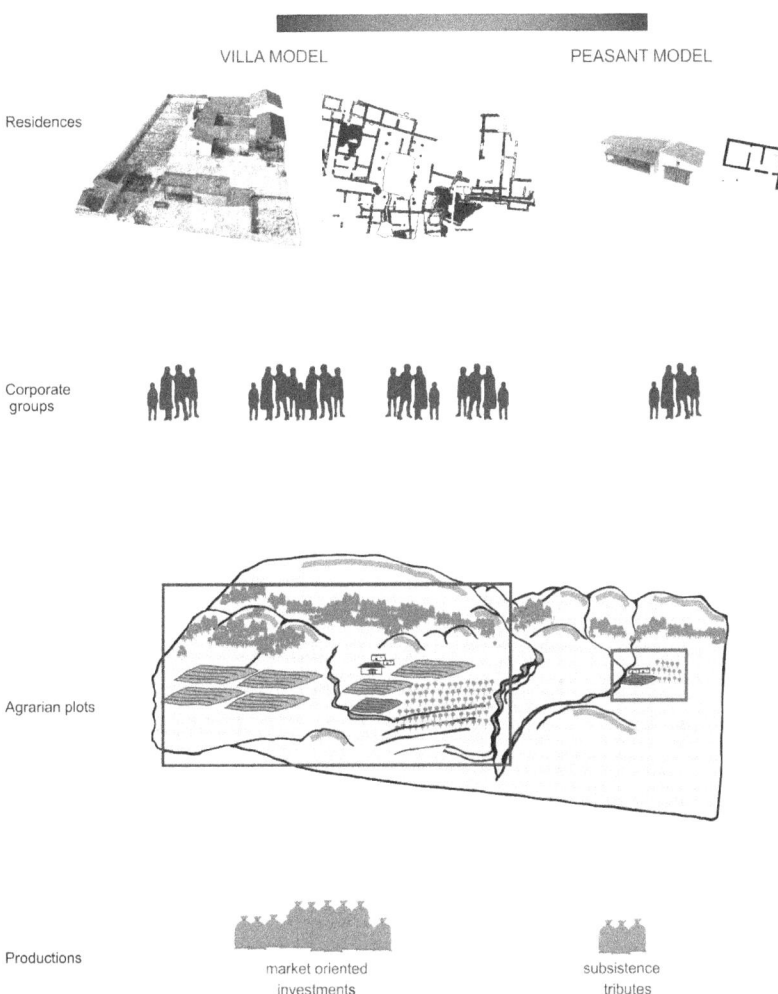

Figure 16 Scheme of the components of the *villa* versus the peasant economic models.

Comparison of case studies related to rural settlements reveals a large morphological diversity in the ways of living. Therefore, it would be useless to attempt to hypothesize a canonical typology like those traditionally established for the study of Roman-period domestic architecture, such as the canonical *villae*. Rather, there was architectural diversity that was conditioned by the adaptation of rural buildings to different socio-environmental factors. It was basically related not just to the agricultural orientation of these settlements, but also to the social structure according to which the domestic activities of the inhabitants of these farms were organized (Rapoport 1969: 46–103).

Nevertheless, this same comparison allows us to detect recurring patterns that can help us better understand the architectural configuration of such settlement. Perhaps the main factor that most rural settlements have in common is their small size. These reduced dimensions suggest that we are dealing with family farms, in which all members of the domestic unit played a fundamental role in the organization of all the economic activities undertaken in these settlements. Whatever their legal status (something that is difficult to infer from the data provided by the archaeological record), the inhabitants of these farms formed a productive unit essentially oriented toward ensuring the subsistence and sustainability of the domestic group. This followed a logic similar to that explained by Chayanov (1925) in his studies of peasant economies. Such family farm would remain within stable margins in terms of composition and scale of production. A household with few members would have been able to mobilize a small workforce, whereas one with many members would have consumed many resources.

As the low productive capacity reflected in the productive features documented in these settlements, small or medium-sized farms would have dominated rural production strategies. Based on the figures of agrarian productivity recorded in the Roman-era treatises *De Re Rustica*, scholars such as P. Ouzoulias and M. Reddé (Ouzoulias 2006: 219, Figure 3; Reddé 2018: 322–323) have proposed that the subsistence margins of a farm of such characteristics could be linked to the exploitation of a plot of land of between 4 and 5 ha. However, these figures would have varied greatly depending on other variables, such as the pedological composition of the plots, the crops grown or alternative economic activities undertaken by the inhabitants of each settlement.

A second recognizable pattern relates to the soil, on which these dwellings are located. In some cases these settlements are in marginal areas, both from a territorial point of view (since rural territories were organized to be dependent on urban centers) and from the perspective of potential agricultural uses. This is the case, for example, with El Cabezo-Clot de Galvany, which is located in an area of the territory of *Ilici* quite a long way, at 15 km from the urban center (Grau and Molina 2013), or with the settlements in the metropolitan area of Madrid (Bermejo Tirado 2017), situated in an interstitial zone close to the borders of the approximated territories (*agri*) of the three main Roman towns (*municipia*) known in the region (Moreno, Brughmans, and Bermejo 2023).

In other cases the marginal nature of some of these farms is determined not so much by the distance from the urban centers as by the poor agricultural potential of the land, on which they are located. This is the case of settlements such as Carrión or Villaemérita in the *ager Emeritensis* that, despite being located in a suburban belt relatively close to *Augusta Emerita*, sit on lands with less agrarian potential than other *villae* in Emerita's territory that were located much farther from the Lusitanian capital (Sánchez Dámaso 2013). This is also the case of the settlements located on the middle course of the Viar River, in the countryside around Sevilla. Their agricultural potential is clearly lower than that of other sectors of the nearby Guadalquivir Valley, or of Cabezo-Clot de Galvany itself, which occupies a zone near some salt flats with little potential from the point of view of agricultural yields (Molina Vidal 2015). Pierre Ouzoulias drew attention to the development of a process of agrarian expansion of lands with little cultivation potential in various sectors of *Gallia Comata* (Ouzoulias 2006). These regions could only be made productive by implementing various intensive agricultural strategies. His thesis was largely endorsed by the results of the Rurland Project (Reddé 2018: 485–501). As we have seen, this marginalist dynamic has also been documented by Institut Català d'Arqueologia Clàssica (ICAC) projects in the high mountainous areas of the Eastern Pyrenees (Palet et al. 2013: 338) and other mid-altitude mountain areas in the Mediterranean region.

But peasants' sites do not always present this marginal aspect, in other cases the preferential location of settlements could be related to intensive farming formulas developed in Roman times. Through an agrarian intensification strategy that involved an increase in farm work, agricultural production per unit of land would have been increased or maintained (Brookfield 1972) and could have taken the form of terrace construction, soil fertilization with domestic waste and irrigation to improve output.

We wish to highlight that peasant structures exhibit a wide variety of frameworks and cannot be strictly reduced to the drudgery-averse strategies proposed by Chayanov, as doing so would exclude certain recognized patterns in Mediterranean peasantry, which is often very intensive. Here, the highly adaptive models of Roman economy fit well, allowing for a diverse range of operational strategies. In our view, the flexibility of peasant locational and organizational models can range from a clear subaltern position, dependent on the state's extractive mechanisms (Wolf 1982), to the idea that intensive agriculture actively resists state intervention (Netting 1993: 61). It is essential to be sensitive to specific contexts when defining forms of peasant integration.

The peasant character of this development of small farms is also reflected in the diversification of production as a subsistence strategy that is documented in many of these habitats. The recurrent presence of various productive facilities related to the processing and storage of products such as cereals or wine is usually accompanied by other smaller facilities linked to domestic stockbreeding, pottery manufacture for local distribution or the exploitation of forest resources. This diversification of small-scale productive activities is one of the most common economic strategies adopted by members of peasant communities in various cultural contexts. It is an attempt to reduce the risks inherent in such agricultural economy. Although they did not engage with evidence from Hispania, the studies of J. M. Frayn (1974, 1979) or, more recently, G. Kron (2017) documented the presence of recommendations on diversification strategies in the context of the classical sources referring to agriculture in Roman Italy.

An overview of rural settlements that takes change over time into account leads to the conclusion that, although the monumental phases of the *villae* are those that have attracted the most scholarly attention, in the majority of cases they only represent a short period of all the occupation sequences recorded in these settlements. In certain sectors of the Iberian interior, the development of these stately residences with their monumental ornamentations can be considered a clearly late Roman phenomenon and, in most cases, limited to the last century of Roman domination.

In many cases the occupation sequence of these settlements is marked by much more humble dwellings that may be compared to other typologies of peasant housing, which have been the subject of previous analysis. In view of these data, one might wonder – in line with the proposals of other scholars with regard to Hispania (Bowes 2014) – if many of the monumental phases of these buildings were the final result of an "agrarian Romanisation" process (Leveau 2014), based on the extension of the slave mode of production that only emerged in the 4th century AD. On the other hand, should we consider it the result of structural changes that affected the local aristocracy, who in the context of the decline of Roman state control in Hispania had been forced to give up functions that had previously been focused on municipal and provincial administration and magistracies? In other words, the chronological comparison of the occupation sequences recorded in many of these rural settlements would not so much be a reflection of the strength of the slave mode of production, but of the decline of an economic system overseen by an imperial aristocracy. The wealth of this aristocracy would have been less the result of its expertise in managing agricultural yields as of their belonging to different lineages privileged by the growing weakness of the late Roman administration.

With this perspective, perhaps we should consider the phenomenon of the end of monumental *villae* as the resilience and sustainability of peasant communities and their ability to adapt to the changing economic and social conditions arising from the collapse of the administration and infrastructure of the late Roman state. They could survive by reusing the resources available in the ruined and unsustainable aristocratic residences that were left in the last moments of Roman imperial domination of the Iberian Peninsula.

References

Allen, M., Lodwick, L., Brindle, T., Fulford, M., & Smith, A. (2017). *New Visions of the Countryside of Roman Britain Volume 2: The Rural Economy of Roman Britain*. London: Society for the Promotion of Roman Studies.

Altieri, M., & Toledo, M. (2011). The agroecological revolution in Latin America: Rescuing nature, ensuring food sovereignty and empowering peasants. *Journal of Peasant Studies*, *38*(3), 587–612.

Ariño, E. (2003). Tipos de campo, modelos de hábitat: Problemas metodológicos e interpretativos de los catastros romanos en Hispania. In M. Prevosti, J. Guitart, & J. M. Palet (eds.), *Territoris antics a la Mediterrània i a la Cossetània oriental*, (pp. 97–116). Barcelona: Generalitat de Catalunya.

Ariño, E. (2006). Modelos de poblamiento rural en la provincia de Salamanca (España) entre la Antigüedad y la Alta Edad Media. *Zephyrus: Revista de prehistoria y arqueología*, *59*, 317–337.

Ariño, E., & Chávez, E. (2019). Las estructuras del campo. In E. Sánchez, & M. Bustamante (eds.), *Arqueología romana en la península Iberica*, (pp. 477–496). Granada: Univ. de Granada.

Ariño, E., & Soto García, M. R. (2016). Técnicas de muestreo en la prospección arqueológica: la experiencia del Ager Salmanticensis (Salamanca, España). *Anales De Arqueología Cordobesa*, *27*, 35–58.

Bagnall, R. S. (2005). Evidence and models for the economy of Roman Egypt. In I. Morris & J. G. Manning (eds.), *The Ancient Economy: Evidence and Models*, (pp. 187–204). Stanford, CA: Stanford University Press.

Bermejo Tirado, J. (2017). Roman peasant habitats and settlement in central Spain (1st c. B.C. – 4th c. A.D.). *Journal of Roman Archaeology*, *30*(1), 351–371.

Bermejo Tirado, J. (2022). Early Imperial Roman peasant communities in central Spain: Agrarian structure, standards of living, and inequality in the north of Roman Carpetania. In J. Bermejo & I. Grau (eds.), *The Archaeology of Peasantry in Roman Spain*, (pp. 47–98). Berlin: De Gruyter.

Bermejo Tirado, J. (2024). Microhistory, archaeological record, and the subaltern debris. *Open Archaeology*, *10*(1), 20240004.

Bermejo Tirado, J., & Grau Mira, I. (Eds.). (2022). *The Archaeology of Peasantry in Roman Spain*. Berlin: De Gruyter.

Bermejo Tirado, J., Moreno Navarro, F., & Colominas, L. (2019). Economías domésticas y patrones de consumo en la villa romana de Fuente Álamo: Estudio comparativo de las fases altoimperial y tardoantigua. In L. Neira

Jiménez (ed.), *Mosaicos romanos en el espacio rural. Investigación y y puesta en valor*, (pp. 239–279). Rome: L'Erma Di Bretschneider

Bintliff, J. L., & Snodgrass, A. M. (1988). Off-site pottery distributions: A regional-interregional perspective. *Current Anthropology*, 29, 506–513.

Boserup, E. (1965). *The Conditions of Agricultural Growth: The Economics of Agrarian Change under Population Pressure*. Chicago, IL: The University of Chicago Press.

Boserup, E. (1981). *Population and Technological Change: A Study of Long-Term Trends*. Chicago, IL: University of Chicago Press.

Bowes, K. (2014). Villas, taxes and trade in fourth century Hispania. In I. Jacobs (ed.), *Production and Prosperity in the Theodosian Period*, (pp. 125–155). Leuven: Peeters.

Bowes, K. (2020). *The Roman Peasant Project 2009–2014: Excavating the Roman Rural Poor*. Ann Arbor: University of Michigan Press.

Bowes, K., & Gutteridge, A. (2005). Rethinking the later Roman landscape. *Journal of Roman Archaeology*, 18, 405–413.

Bowman, A. (2009). Quantifying Egyptian agriculture. In A. Bowman & A. Wilson (eds.), *Quantifying the Roman Economy: Methods and Problems*, (pp. 177–204). Oxford: Oxford University Press.

Bowman, A., & Wilson, A. (eds.). (2009). *Quantifying the Roman Economy: Methods and Problems*. Oxford: Oxford University Press.

Brogiolo, G. P., & Chavarría Arnau, A. (2008). *Aristocrazie e Campagne nell'Occidente de Costantino a Carlo Magno*. Florencia: All'Insegna del Gilio.

Brookfield, H. C. (1972). Intensification and disintensification in Pacific agriculture: A theoretical approach. *Pacific Viewpoint*, 13, 30–48.

Brookfield, H. C. (1984). Intensification revisited. *Pacific Viewpoint*, 25, 15–44. https://doi.org/10.1111/apv.251002.

Brughmans, T., & Poblome, J. (2016). Roman bazaar or market economy? Explaining tableware distributions through computational modelling. *Antiquity*, 350, 393–408.

Capogrossi Colognesi, L. (1981). Proprietà agraria e lavoro subordinato nei giuristi e degli agronomi tra repubblica e principato. In A. Giardina & A. Schiavone (eds.), *Società romana e produzione schiavistica: 1. L'Italia: Insediamenti e Forme Economiche*, (pp. 445–454). Rome: Laterza.

Carandini, A. (1985). *Settefinestre: Una villa schiavistica nell'Etruria romana*. Parma: Panini.

Carandini, A. (1989). La villa romana e la piantagione schiavistica. In E. Gabba & A. Schiavone (eds.), *Storia di Roma IV: Caratteri e Morfologie*, (pp. 101–192). Turin: Einaudi.

Carneiro, A. (2020). Adapting to change in rural Lusitania: Zooarchaeological record in the Horta da Torre Roman villa (Portugal). *European Journal of Postclassical Archaeologies*, *10*, 247–278.

Carvalho, P. (2007). *Cova da Beira: Ocupação e exploração do território na época romana (um território rural no interior norte da Lusitânia)*. Coimbra: Cámara Municipal de Fundao.

Casas i Genover, J., Castanyer, P., Nolla, J. M., & Tremoleda, J. (1995). *El Món rural d'Època romana a Catalunya: L'Exemple del nord-est*. Girona: Centre d'Investigacions Arqueològiques de Girona.

Castrorao Barba, A. (2020). *La fine delle ville romane in Italia tra Tarda Antichità e Alto Medioevo (III-VIII secolo)*. Bari: Edipuglia.

Chaouali, M. (2002). Les nundinae dans les grands domaines en Afrique du Nord à l'époque romaine. *Antiquités africaines*, *38–39*, 375–386.

Chavarría, A., Arce, J., & Brogiolo, G. (eds.). (2006). *Villas Tardoantiguas en el Mediterráneo Occidental*. Madrid: Consejo Superior de Investigaciones Científicas.

Chavarría Arnau, A. (2007). *El final de las "villae" en "Hispania" (siglos IV-VII D.C.)*. Turnhout: Brepols.

Chayanov, A. V. (1925). *Organizatsiya krest'yanskogo khozyaystva* [Organization of the Peasant Farm]. Moscow: Kooperativnoe izdatel'stvo.

Chérif, A., & González Bordas, H. (2020). Henchir Hnich (région du Krib, Tunisie): la découverte de la première copie de la *lex Hadriana de agris rudibus* et de trois inscriptions funéraires inédites. In S. Aounallah & A. Mastino (eds.), *L'epigrafia del Nord Africa: novità, riletture, nuove sintesi* (Epigrafia e antichità 45), (pp. 205–221). Faenza: Fratelli Lega Editori.

Colominas, L., Palet, J. M., & Garcia-Molsosa, A. (2020). What happened in the highlands? Characterising Pyrenean livestock practices during the transition from the Iron Age to the Roman period. *Archaeological and Anthropological Sciences*, *12*, 69–80.

Curchin, L. (1985). Vici and pagi in Roman Spain. *Revue des Études Anciennes*, *87*(3–4), 327–343.

De Ligt, L. (1990). Demand, supply, distribution: The Roman peasantry between town and countryside: Rural monetization and peasant demand. *Münstersche Beiträge zur antiken Handelsgeschichte*, *9*(2), 24–56.

De Ligt, L. (1991). The Roman peasantry demand, supply, distribution between town and countryside II: Supply, distribution and a comparative perspective. *Münstersche Beiträge zur antiken Handelsgeschichte*, *10*(1), 33–77.

De Ligt, L. (1993). *Fairs and Markets in the Roman Empire: Economic and Social Aspects of Periodic Trade in a Pre-industrial society*. Leiden: Brill.

De Ligt, L. (1998). Studies in legal and agrarian history I: The inscription from Henchir-Mettich and the lex Manciana. *Ancient Society*, *29*, 219–239.

De Neeve, P. W. (1984). *Colonus: Private Farm-tenancy in Roman Italy during the Republic and the Early Principate*. Amsterdam: J. C. Gieben.

De Vos, M. (2001). *Rus Africum: Terra, acqua, olio nell'Africa settentrionale: Scavo e ricognizione nei dintorni di Dougga (Alto Tell Tunisino)*. Trento: Università degli Studi di Trento.

Delgado Torres, M., & Jaén, D. (2016). El Conjunto Arqueológico de Fuente Álamo (Puente Genil, Córdoba). Quince años de puesta en valor y gestión integral del patrimonio en el medio rural. In D. Vaquerizo Gil (ed.), *Rescate. Del registro arqueológico a la sociedad del conocimiento: El patrimonio arqueológico como agente de desarrollo sostenible*, (pp. 223–256). Córdoba: Universidad de Córdoba.

Delgado Torres, M., & Jaén, D. (2019). La Fuente del Álamo: Historia y arqueología de un lugar excepcional (Puente Genil, Córdoba). In L. Neira Jiménez (ed.), *Mosaicos romanos en el espacio rural. Investigación y puesta en valor*, (pp. 219–238). Rome: L'Erma di Bretschneider.

D'Encarnaçao, J., Cardoso, G., & Almeida, M. M. (eds.). (2020). *Villae romanas: Investigaçao e inovaçao*. Cascais: Câmara Municipal de Cascais.

Diarte-Blasco, P. (2018). *Late Antique & Early Medieval Hispania: Landscapes without Strategy? An Archaeological Approach*. Oxford: Oxbow Books.

Dodd, J. (2019). A conceptual framework to approaching late antique villa transformational trajectories. *Journal of Ancient History and Archaeology*, *6*(4), 30–44.

Domergue, C. (1990). *Les Mines de la péninsule Ibérique dans l'Antiquité romaine*. Rome: EFR.

Dossey, L. (2010). *Peasant and Empire in Christian North Africa*. Berkeley: University of California Press.

Edelman, M. (2013). What is a peasant? What are peasantries? A briefing paper on issues of definition. *Journal of Peasant Studies*, *40*(1), 1–18.

Ejarque, A., Julià, R., Riera, S., et al. (2009). Tracing the history of highland human management in the Eastern Pre-Pyrenees (Spain): An interdisciplinary approach. *The Holocene*, *19*(8), 1241–1255.

Ellis, F. (1988a). *Peasant Economics: Farm Households and Agrarian Development*. Cambridge: Cambridge University Press.

Ellis, S. P. (1988b). The end of the Roman house. *American Journal of Archaeology*, *92*(4), 565–576. https://doi.org/10.2307/505251.

Erdkamp, P. (1999). Agriculture, underemployment, and the cost of rural labour in the Roman world. *Classical Quarterly*, *49*(2), 556–572.

Erdkamp, P. (2005). *The Grain Market in the Roman Empire: A Social, Political and Economic Study.* Cambridge: Cambridge University Press.

Euba, I., & Palet, J. M. (2010). L'exploitation des ressources végétales dans les Pyrénées orientales durant l'Holocène: Analyse anthracologique des structures d'élevage, de fours et de charbonnières dans l'Alt Urgell (chaîne du Cadí) et la vallée du Madriu (Andorre). *Quaternaire, 21*(3), 305–316.

Evans, J. K. (1980a). Plebs Rustica: The peasantry of classical Italy. *American Journal of Ancient History, 5*(1), 19–47.

Evans, J. K. (1980b). *Plebs Rustica*: The peasantry of classical Italy II. *American Journal of Ancient History, 5*(2), 134–173.

Fabião, C. (2002). Os chamados castella do Sudoeste: Arquitectura, cronología e funções. *Archivo Español de Arqueología, 75,* 177–193.

Ferdière, A. (2015). Essai de typologie des greniers ruraux de Gaule du Nord. *Revue archéologique du Centre de la France,* 54. https://journals.openedition.org/racf/2294.

Fernández Castro, M. C. (1982). *Villas romanas en España.* Madrid: Ministerio de Cultura.

Fernández Ochoa, C., Gil Sendino, F., & Orejas Saco del Valle, A. (2004). La villa romana de Veranes: El complejo rural tardorromano y propuesta de estudio del territorio. *Archivo Español de Arqueología, 77,* 197–220.

Fernández Flores, A., & Carrasco Gómez, I. (2013–2014). Los asentamientos rurales romanos del curso medio del río Viar (Sevilla). *Romula, 12–13,* 95–124.

Fernández Ochoa, C., García-Entero, V., & Gil Sendino, F. (2008). *Las villae tardorromanas en el occidente del Imperio: Arquitectura y función* (IV Coloquio Internacional de Arqueología en Gijón). Gijón: Ayto de Gijón.

Fernández Ochoa, C., Gil Sendino, F., & Orejas Saco del Valle, A. (2004). La villa romana de Veranes: El complejo rural tardorromano y propuesta de estudio del territorio. *Archivo Español de Arqueología, 77,* 197–220.

Fernández Ochoa, C., Salido, J., & Zarzalejos, M. (2014). Las formas de ocupación rural en Hispania: Entre la terminología y la praxis arqueológica. *Cuadernos de Prehistoria y Arqueología de la UAM, 40,* 111–136.

Fiches, J. L., Plana, R., & Revilla, V. (eds.). (2013). *Paysages ruraux et territoires dans les cités de l'Occident romain: Gallia et Hispania.* Montpellier: Presses Universitaires de la Méditerranée.

Finley, M. I. (1976). Private farm tenancy in Italy before Diocletian. In M. I. Finley (ed.), *Studies in Roman Property,* (pp. 103–121). Cambridge: Cambridge University Press.

Flórez, M., & Palet, J. M. (2012). Análisis arqueomorfológico y dinámica territorial en el Vallés Oriental (Barcelona) de la Protohistoria (s. VI-V a.C.) a la alta

Edad Media. *Archivo Espanol de Arqueologia*, *85*, 167–192. https://doi.org/10.3989/aespa.085.012.010.

Foxhall, L. (1990). The dependent tenant: Land leasing and labour in Italy and Greece. *Journal of Roman Studies*, *80*, 97–114.

Francovich, R., & Hodges, R. (2003). *Villa to Village: The Transformation of the Roman Countryside*. Oxford: Duckworth.

Frayn, J. M. (1974). Subsistence farming in Italy during the Roman period: A preliminary discussion of the evidence. *Greece & Rome*, *21*(1), 11–18. https://doi.org/10.1017/S0017383500021628.

Frayn, J. M. (1979). *Subsistence Farming in Roman Italy*. London: Centaur Press Limited.

Frías, C. (2010). *El poblamiento rural de Dianium, Lucentum, Ilici y la ciudad romana de la Vila Joiosa (siglos II a. C.-VII d. C.)*. Alicante: Ed. Univ. Alicante.

Gallant, T. W. (1991). *Risk and Survival in Ancient Greece*. New York: Polity Place.

García Sánchez, J., & Carneiro, A. (2021). El Castelo do Mau Vizinho, Arraiolos: Documentación y revisión de un contexto de la romanización. *Spal*, *30*(1), 290–309.

García Sánchez, J., & Cisneros, M. (2013). An off-site approach to late iron age and roman landscapes on the Northern Plateau, Spain. *European Journal of Archaeology*, *16*(2), 289–313.

Garnsey, P. (1976). Peasants in ancient Roman society. *Journal of Peasant Studies*, *3*(2), 221–235.

Garnsey, P. (1979). Where did Italian peasants live? *Proceedings of the Cambridge Philological Society*, *25*, 1–25.

Garnsey, P. (ed.). (1980). *Non-slave labour in the Greco-Roman world* (Cambridge Philological Society Supplementary Volume 6). Cambridge: Cambridge University Press.

Gerritsen, P. (2002). *Diversity at Stake: A Farmer's Perspective on Biodiversity and Conservation in Western Mexico*. Wageningen Studies on Heterogeneity and Relocalisation 4, Wageningen: Wageningen University.

Gerritsen, P. (2012). "Diversity (still) at stake": A farmers' perspective on biodiversity and conservation in Western Mexico. In B. Arts, S. van Bommel, M. Ros-Tonen, & G. Verschoor (eds.), *Forest-People Interfaces*, (pp. 171–186). Wageningen: Wageningen Academic.

Giardina, A., & Schiavone, A. (eds.) (1981). *Società romana e produzione schiavistica*. 3 Vols. Rome: Laterza.

González Bordas, H. (2020). Alcune considerazioni sulla portata della *lex Hadriana de agris rudibus*. In C. Soraci (ed.), *Fiscalità ed epigrafia nel mondo romano: Atti del convegno internazionale (Catania, 28-29 giugno 2019)*, (pp. 61–76). Roma: Bibliotheca Aperta 1.

González Bordas, H., & France, J. (2017). A new edition of the imperial regulation from the Lella Drebblia site near Dougga (AE, 2001, 2083). *Journal of Roman Archaeology, 30*, 407–428.

Gorges, J.-G. (1979). *Les villas hispano-romaines: Inventaire et problématique archéologiques*. Bordeaux: Université de Bordeaux.

Grau Mira, I. (2014). The rural landscape of the Valley of Alcoi in the eastern Iberian Iron Age: agricultural intensification and sociopolitical dynamics. *Journal of Field Archaeology, 39*(2), 124–133.

Grau Mira, I. (2022). A peasant landscape in the Eastern Roman Spain: An archaeological approach to territorial organization and economic models. In Bermejo, J. & Grau-Mira, I. (eds.), *The Archaeology of Peasantry in Roman Spain*, (pp. 91–110). Berlín: De Gruyter.

Grau Mira, I., Amorós López, I., & Segura, J. M. (2017). *El santuario ibérico y romano de La Serreta. Prácticas rituales y paisaje en el área central de la Contestania*. Alcoi: Museu d'Alcoi.

Grau Mira, I., Gutiérrez-Rodríguez, M., López Sáez, J., et al. (2023). Las terrazas romanas de Ull de Canals (Banyeres de Mariola, Alacant). Aproximación espacial, geoarqueológica y bioarqueológica a las estrategias agrarias. In I. Grau, et al. (eds.), *Paisajes romanos en el sur de la Provincia Tarraconense. Análisis arqueológico de la estructura territorial y el modelo socioeconómico*, (pp. 91–126). Alicante: Publicacions Universitat d'Alacant.

Grau Mira, I., Gutiérrez-Rodríguez, M., López, J. A. et al. (2024). Roman farmers in eastern Iberia: A spatial, geoarchaeological and bioarchaeological approach to agrarian strategies. *Quaternary International, 699*, 4–22.

Grau Mira, I., Jimenez, H., & Sarabia, J. (2021). Arqueología de los espacios y comunidades agrarias desde el registro superficial: un análisis comparado de paisajes y prácticas rurales desde la Antigüedad al Medievo. In V. Mayoral, I. Grau, & J. P. Bellón (eds.), *Arqueología y sociedad de los espacios agrarios: en busca de la gente invisible a través de la materialidad del paisaje*, (pp. 27–46). Madrid: CSIC.

Grau Mira, I., & Molina, J. (2013). *Diversité territoriale et modèles d'exploitation aux paysages ruraux du Sud de la Tarraconense (ss. II av.-II apr.)*. In J. L. Fiches, R. Plana, & V. Revilla (eds.), *Paysages ruraux et territoires dans les cités de l'Occident romain*, (pp. 53–60). Montpellier: Presses Universitaires de La Méditerranée.

Halstead, P. (1987). Traditional and ancient rural economy in Mediterranean Europe: plus ça change? *Journal of Hellenic Studies, 107*, 77–87.

Halstead, P. (2014). *Two Oxen Ahead: Pre-mechanized Farming in the Mediterranean*. Chichester: Wiley-Blackwell.

Hidalgo, R. (ed.), (2016). *Las villas romanas de la Bética*. 2 Vols. Sevilla: Univ. Sevilla.

Hirth, K. (2020). *The Organization of Ancient Economies: A Global Perspective*. Cambridge: Cambridge University Press.

Hobsbawm, E. J. (1973). Peasants and politics. *The Journal of Peasant Studies*, *1*(1), 3–22.

Hodkinson, S. (1988). Animal husbandry in the Greek polis. In C. R. Whittaker (ed.), *Pastoral Economies in Classical Antiquity*, (pp. 35–74). Cambridge: Cambridge University Press.

Járrega, R., & Berni, P. (2016). *Amphorae ex Hispania: paisajes de producción y consumo. Amphorae ex Hispania: paisajes de producción y consumo*. Tarragona: ICAC.

Kasprzyk, M. (2018). L'équipement et les formes des établissements ruraux du Bas-Empire. In M. Reddé (ed.), *Gallia Rustica 2: Les Campagnes du nord-est de la Gaule de la fin de l'âge du Fer à l'Antiquité Tardive*, (pp. 235–305). Bordeaux: Ausonius Editions.

Kehoe, D. (1984). Private and imperial management of Roman estates in North Africa. *Law and History Review*, *2*(2), 241–263.

Kehoe, D. (1988). *The Economics of Agriculture in Roman Imperial Estates in North Africa*. Göttingen: Vandenhoeck & Ruprecht.

Knitter, D., & Nakoinz, O. (2018). The relative concentration of interaction – a proposal for an integrated understanding of centrality and central places. *Land*, *7*(3), 1–18.

Kolendo, J. (1991). *Le colonat en Afrique romaine sous le Haut-Empire*. Paris: Les Belles Lettres.

Kron, G. (2017). The diversification and intensification of Italian agriculture: The complementary roles of the small and wealthy farmer. In T. C. A. De Haas & G. Tol (eds.), *The Economic Integration of Roman Italy: Rural Communities in a Globalizing World*, (pp. 112–140). Leiden: Brill.

Le Roux, P. (2009). Le pagus dans la péninsule ibérique. *Chiron*, *39*, 19–44.

Launaro, A. (2011). *Peasants and Slaves: The Rural Population of Roman Italy (200 BC to AD 100)*. Cambridge: Cambridge University Press.

Launaro, A. (2015). The nature of the villa economy. In P. Erdkamp, K. Verboven, & A. Zuiderhoek (eds.), *Ownership and Exploitation of Land and Natural Resources in the Roman World*, (pp. 173–186). Oxford: Oxford University Press.

Leveau, P. (2014). Villa, Romanisation, Développement Économique Entre Idéal-Type Wébérien et Modélisation Territoriale. In C. Apicella, M.-L. Haack, & F. Lerouxel (eds.), *Les affaires de Monsieur Andreau: Économie et société du monde romain*, (pp. 97–106). Bordeaux: De Boccard.

Leveau, Ph., & Palet, J. M. (2010). Les Pyrénées romaines, la frontière, la ville et la montagne: L'apport de l'archéologie du paysage. *Pallas*, *82*, 171–198.

Levi, M. (1988). *Of Rule and Revenue*. Los Angeles: University of California Press.

López Medina, M. J. (2020). La alimentación en las unidades domésticas campesinas a partir de las Metamorfosis de Ovidio. *Gerión*, *38*(1), 117–135.

López Palomo, L. A. (2013–2014). Balneum y villa: La secuencia romana de Fuente Álamo (Puente Génil, Córdoba). *Romula*, 12–13, 295–348.

Martin, R. (1971). *Recherches sur les agronomes latins et leurs conceptions économiques et sociales*. Paris: Les Belles Lettres.

Martin, S. (2019). Storage in a Non-Villa Landscape: The Batavian Countryside. In S. Martin (ed.), *Rural Granaries in Northern Gaul (Sixth Century BCE – Fourth Century CE): From Archaeology to Economic History*, (pp. 106–121). Leiden: Brill.

Martínez, R., Nogales, T., & Rodà, I. (coord.) (2020). *Actas del Congreso Internacional Las Villas romanas bajoimperiales de Hispania (Palencia 2016)*. Palencia: Dip. de Palencia.

Mayer, M., & Olesti, O. (2001). La *sortitio* de *Ilici*. Del documento epigráfico al paisaje histórico. *Dialogues d'Histoire Ancienne*, *27*(1), 109–130.

Mayoral, V. (2018). *Fortificaciones, recintos ciclópeos y proceso de romanización el la comarca natural de La Serena: Siglos II a.C al I d.C*. Mérida: IAM.

Mayoral, V., Bustamante, M., Martínez del Pozo J. Á. et al. (2014). Los paisajes agrarios de la romanización en el Suroeste peninsular: balance de los últimos trabajos desarrollados desde el Instituto de Arqueología. In *Actas del VI Encuentro de Arqueología del Suroeste Peninsular*, (pp. 1389–1423). Badajoz: Ayuntamiento de Villafranca de los Barros.

Mayoral, V., Grau, I., & Bellón, J. P. (eds.). (2021). *Arqueología y Sociedad de los Paisajes Agrarios: En Busca de la Gente Invisible a Través de la Materialidad*. In *Anejos de Archivo Español de Arqueología XCI* (pp. 61–79). Madrid: CSIC.

Mintz, S. W. (1973). A Note on the Definition of Peasantries. *Journal of Peasant Studies*, *1*(1), 91–106.

Molina Vidal, J. (2011). La villa romana: de las fuentes escritas a la creación del concepto histórico. In V. Revilla, J. R. González, & M. Prevosti (eds.), *Actes del simposi les vil·les romanes a la tarraconense. Implantació, evolució i trasformació: Estat actual de la investigació del món rural en època romana*, (pp. 37–48). Lleida: MAC.

Molina Vidal, J. (2015). Poblamiento rural en el territorium de Ilici: la granja romana de El Cabezo-Clot de Galvany (Elx, Alacant). *Sagvntvm. Papeles Del Laboratorio De Arqueología De Valencia*, *47*, 105–120. https://doi.org/10.7203/SAGVNTVM.47.3926.

Montevecchi, O. (1950). *I contratti di lavoro e di servizio nell'Egitto greco-romano e bizantino*. Milan: Vita e Pensiero.

Moreno, F., Brughmans, T., & Bermejo, J. (2023). Exploring economic integration of peasant settlements in Roman Central Spain (1st c. – 3rd c. AD). *Journal of Archaeological Science: Reports*, *51*, 104106.

Moret, P. (2004). *Tours de Guet, Maisons à Tour et Petits Établissements Fortifiés de l'Hispanie Républicaine: L'apport des Sources Littéraires*. In P. Moret & T. Chapa Brunet (eds.), *Torres, Atalayas y Casas Fortificadas: Explotación y Control del Territorio en Hispania (s. III a.C. – s. I d.C.)*, (pp. 13–30). Jaén: Universidad de Jaén.

Moret, P. (2010). *Les Tours Rurales et les Maisons Fortes de l'Hispanie Romaine: Éléments pour un Bilan*. In V. Mayoral & S. Celestino (eds.), *Los Paisajes Rurales de la Romanización: Arquitectura y Explotación del Territorio*, (pp. 9–36). Madrid: La Ergástula Ediciones.

Moret, P. (2016). Les Tours Isolées de l'Hispanie Romaine: Postes Militaires ou Maisons Fortes. In S. Müth, P. I. Schneider, M. Scanelle, & P. D. de Staebler (eds.), *Focus on Fortifications*, (pp. 456–468). Oxford: Oxbow Books.

Morín, J., Barroso R., Escolà, M. et al. (2003). La Gravera de l'Eugeni (Artesa de Lleida): una cabaña de época romana. *Bolskan*, *20*, 163–175.

Narotzky, S. (2016). Where have all the peasants gone? *Annual Review of Anthropology*, *45*, 1–18.

Netting, R. McC. (1993). *Smallholders, Householders: Farm Families and the Ecology of Intensive, Sustainable Agriculture*. Stanford, CA: Stanford University Press.

Noguera Celdrán, J. M., & Antolinos Marín, J. A. (2009). Áreas productivas y zonas de servicio en la villa romana de Los Cipreses (Jumilla, Murcia). *Archivo Español de Arqueología*, *82*, 191–220.

Olesti, O., Narbarte, J., Iriarte, E., & Carrillo, B. (2024). La construcción de los campos en un sistema centuriado. La aplicación de la geoarqueología en la centuriación de Ilici (Elche, Alicante). *Agri Centuriati, An International Journal of Landscape Archaeology*, *21*, 9–32.

Orejas, A., & Sánchez Palencia, F. J. (2002). Mines, territorial organization, and social structure in Roman Iberia: Carthago Noua and the peninsular northwest. *American Journal of Archaeology*, *106*(4), 581–599.

Orejas A., & Sastre I. (1999). Fiscalité et organisation du territoire dans le Nord-Ouest de la péninsule Ibérique: civitates, tribut et ager mensura conprehensus. *Dialogues d' Histoire Ancienne, 25*(1), 159–188.

Ouzoulias, P. (2006). *L'économie agraire de la Gaule: aperçus historiographiques et perspectives archéologiques*, Doctorat, Université de Franche-Comté École doctorale Langages, espaces, temps, sociétés, Besançon.

Palet, J. M., Orengo, H. A., Ejarque, A. et al. (2013). Arqueología de paisajes altimontanos pirenaicos: formas de explotación y usos del medio en época romana en valle del Madriu-Perafita-Claror (Andorra) y en la Sierra del Cadí (Alt Urgell). In J. L. Fiches, R. Plana-Mallart, & V. Revilla Calvo (eds.), *Paysages ruraux et territoires dans les cités de l'Occident romain: Gallia et Hispania*, (pp. 329–340). Montpellier: Presses universitaires de la Méditerranée.

Patón Lorca, B. (2001). La mansión de Materno. In D. Fernández-Galiano (ed.), *Carranque: Centro de Hispania romana*, (pp. 83–91). Guadalajara: Museo Arqueológico Regional.

Picado, Y. (2004). Nuevos datos para el conocimiento del área periurbana de Mérida en época altoimperial: la villa de Carrión. Intervención arqueológica realizada en el trazado de la Autovía de la Plata (tramo Mérida-Almendralejo Sur). *Mérida. Excavaciones arqueológicas, 7*, 231–246.

Poirier, N. (2016). Archaeological evidence for agrarian manuring: Studying the time-space dynamics of agricultural areas with surface-collected off-site material. In J. Klápště (ed.), *Agrarian Technology in the Medieval Landscape*, (pp. 279–290). Turnhout: Bretpol.

Ponsich, M. (1998). *Aceite de oliva y salazones de pescado: Factores geoeconómicos de Bética y Tingitania*. Madrid: UCM.

Prevosti, M., & Guitart, J. (eds.) (2011). *Ager Tarraconensis 2. El poblament*. Tarragona: ICAC.

Quirós Castillo, J. A. (2020). *Do we need an archaeology of peasantries? A new look at rural history (at light of the Iberian experience)*. In J. A. Quirós Castillo (ed.), *Archaeology and History of Peasantries 1: From the Late Prehistory to the Middle Ages*, (pp. 23–40). Vitoria: Universidad del País Vasco.

Quirós Castillo, J. A. (2022). From villa to village? Relational approaches within Roman and Medieval Iberian rural societies. In J. Bermejo Tirado & I. Grau Mira (ed.), *The Archaeology of Peasantry in Roman Spain*, (pp. 253–276). Berlin: De Gruyter.

Rapoport, A. (1969). *House Form and Culture*. Englewood Cliffs, NJ: Prentice-Hall.

Reddé, M., dir. (2018). *Gallia Rustica: Les campagnes du nord-est de la Gaule, de la fin de l'Âge du fer à l'Antiquité tardive*, T2. Bordeaux: Ed. Ausonius.

Remesal, J. (2008). La villa como sistema económico. In V. Revilla, J. R. González, & M. Prevosti (eds.), *Actes del simposi les vil·les romanes a la tarraconense. Implantació, evolució i trasformació: Estat actual de la investigació del món rural en època romana*, (pp. 49–54). Lleida: MAC.

Remesal, J. (2016). De re rustica Baeticae. In R. Hidalgo Prieto (coord.), *Las villas romanas de la Bética*. (Vol. 1, pp. 27–38). Sevilla: Ed. de Sevilla.

Remesal, J., Revilla, V., & Martí Oliveras, A. (2019). *Paisajes productivos y redes comerciales en el Imperio Romano = Productive landscapes and trade networks in the Roman Empire*. Barcelona: Ed. Univ. de Barcelona.

Revilla, V. (2022). On the margins of the villa system? Rural architecture and socioeconomic strategies in North-Eastern Roman Spain. In J. Bermejo & I. Grau-Mira (eds.), *The Archaeology of Peasantry in Roman Spain*, (pp. 169–200). Berlín: De Gruyter.

Ruiz del Árbol, M. (2005). *La arqueología de los espacios cultivados: terrazas y su explotación agraria romana en un área de montaña: la Sierra de Francia*. Anejos de Archivo Español de Arqueología XXXVI. Madrid: CSIC.

Ruiz del Árbol, M. (2006). Los paisajes agrarios del NE de Lusitania: terrazas y explotación agraria romanas en la Sierra de Francia. *Arqueología Espacial*, 26, 115–142.

Sánchez Barrero, P. D. (2013). El paisaje agrario romano en las proximidades de Augusta Emerita. In J. L. Fiches, R. Plana-Mallart, & V. Revilla Calvo (eds.), *Paysages ruraux et territoires dans les cités de l'Occident romain: Gallia et Hispania*, (pp. 293–301). Montpellier: Presses universitaires de la Méditerranée.

Sánchez-Palencia, J., & Currás, B. (2021). Arqueología de los espacios agrarios en las zonas mineras romanas del noreste de Lusitania: la Sierra de la Peña de Francia (Salamanca). In V. Mayoral, I. Grau, & J. P. Bellón (ed.), *Arqueología y sociedad de los espacios agrarios: en busca de la gente invisible a través de la materialidad del paisaje*, (pp. 79–92). Madrid: CSIC.

Sánchez-Simón, M. (2022). Villae and farms: Early imperial rural settlement in the Adaja-Eresma Basin (Central Roman Spain). In J. Bermejo Tirado & I. Mira (eds.), *The Archaeology of Peasantry in Roman Spain*, (pp. 201–228). Berlin: De Gruyter. https://doi.org/10.1515/9783110757415-010.

Sastre, I. (2007). Campesinado, escritura y paisaje: algunas cuestiones sobre el mundo provincial romano occidental. *Gerión*, 25, N° Extra 1, 375–382.

Scheidel, W., Morris I., & Saller R. (ed.), (2007). *The Cambridge Economic History of the Greco-Roman World*. Cambridge: Cambridge University Press.

Scott, J. C. (1998). *Seeing Like a State: How Certain Schemes to Improve the Human Condition Have Failed*. New Haven, CT: Yale University Press.

Scott, J. C. (2009). *The Art of Not Being Governed: An Anarchist History of Upland Southeast Asia*. New Haven, CT: Yale University Press.

Shanin, T. (1971a). Peasantry: Delineation of a sociological concept and field of study. In T. Shanin (ed.), *Peasants and Peasant Societies: Selected Readings*, (pp. 5–21). Harmondsworth: Penguin Books.

Shanin, T. (1971b). Peasantry: Delineation of a sociological concept and field of study. *European Journal of Sociology, 12*(2), 289–300.

Shanin, T. (1990). *Defining Peasants: Essays Concerning Rural Societies, Expolary Economies and Learning from Them in the Contemporary World*. Oxford: Blackwell.

Shaw, B. D. (2015). *Bringing in the Sheaves: Economy and Metaphor in the Roman World*. Toronto: University of Toronto Press.

Sinner A., & Carreras, C. (2019). Methods of palaeodemography: The case of the Iberian oppida and the Roman cities of North-East Spain. *Oxford Journal of Archaeology, 38*(3), 302–324.

Sinner, A., & Revilla, V. (ed.). (2022). *Religious Dynamics in a Microcontinent: Cult Places, Identities and Cultural Change in Hispania*. Turnhout: Bretpols.

Smith, A. T., Allen, M. G., Brindle, T., & Fulford, M. (2016). *New Visions of the Countryside of Roman Britain Volume 1: The Rural Settlement of Roman Britain*. Bristol: The Society for the Promotion of Roman Studies.

Smith, A. T., Allen, M. G., Brindle, T. et al. (2018). *New Visions of the Countryside of Roman Britain Volume 3: Life and Death in the Countryside of Roman Britain*. Bristol: The Society for the Promotion of Roman Studies.

Stek, T. (2009). *Cult Places and Cultural Change in Republican Italy: A Contextual Approach to Religious Aspects of Rural Society after the Roman Conquest*. Amsterdam: Amsterdam University Press.

Stone, D. (1998). Culture and investment in the rural landscape: The North African bonus agricola. *Antiquités Africaines, 29*, 103–113.

Tarpin M. (2002): *Vici et pagi dans l'Occident romain*. Rome: Collection de l'École Française de Rome.

Teichner, F. (2008). *Entre tierra y mar = Zwischen Land und Meer: Architektur und Wirtschaftsweise ländlicher Siedlungsplätze im Süden der römischen Provinz Lusitanien (Portugal)*. Mérida: Museo Nacional de Arte Romano.

Teichner, F. (2013). El territorium de Ossonoba (Lusitania): Economía agrícola y economía «marítima». In J. L. Fiches, R. Plana, & V. Revilla (eds.), *Paysages ruraux et territoires dans les cités de l'Occident romain*, (pp. 137–148). Montpellier: Presses Universitaires de La Méditerranée.

Tejerizo, C. (2012). Early medieval household archaeology in Northwest Iberia (6th–11th centuries). *Arqueología de la Arquitectura, 9*, 181–194.

Tejerizo García, C., Carvajal Castro, Á., Marín Suárez, C., Martínez Álvarez, C., & Mansilla, R. (2015). La construcción histórica de los paisajes en el sector central de la cuenca del Duero: primeros resultados de una prospección intensiva. *Territorio, sociedad y poder: revista de estudios medievales, 10*, 39–62.

Temin, P. (2013). *The Roman Market Economy*. New York: Princeton University Press.

Theng, B. (2021). Finding the social life of rural non-elites in Roman Italy. *Theoretical Roman Archaeology Journal, 4*(1), 1–32.

Toledo, V. M. (1990). The ecological rationality of peasant production. In M. Altieri & S. Hecht (eds.), *Agroecology and Small Farmer Development*, (pp. 51–58). Boca Raton, FL: CRC Press.

Van der Ploeg, J. D. (2008). *The New Peasantries: Rural Development in Times of Globalization*. London: Routledge.

Van der Ploeg, J. D. (2015). *El campesinado y el arte de la agricultura*. Barcelona: Icaria.

Vigil-Escalera, A. (2012). Apuntes sobre la arquitectura de los hogares y hornos domésticos altomedievales del centro de la península Ibérica (siglos V-VIII d. C.). In J. A. Quirós (ed.), *Arqueología de la arquitectura y arquitectura del espacio doméstico en la alta Edad Media Europea* (Monográfico Revista Arqueología de la Arquitectura, (pp. 165–180). Madrid: CSIC.

Villaseca, A., & Adiego. P. (2000). El centre de producció ceràmica de les Planes de Roquis, Reus (Baix Camp). *Documents d'Arqueologia Clàssica, 3*, 275–284.

Wickham, C. (2005). *Framing the Early Middle Ages: Europe and the Mediterranean 400–800*. Oxford: Oxford University Press.

Witcher, R. E. (2012). "That from a long way off look like farms": The classification of Roman rural sites. In P. J. Attema & G. Schörner (eds.), *Comparative Issues in the Archaeology of the Roman Rural Landscape* (Journal of Roman Archaeology Suppl. 88, (pp. 11–30)). Portsmouth, RI: JRA.

Wolf, E. R. (1966). *Peasants* (Foundations of Modern Anthropology Series). Englewood Cliffs, NJ: Prentice-Hall.

Wolf, E. R. (1982). *Europe and the People without History*. Los Angeles: University of California Press.

Acknowledgments

This Element is the outcome of research and reflections developed over recent years in collaboration with numerous colleagues, too many to enumerate in a comprehensive list. Nevertheless, we believe it is appropriate to acknowledge the contributions of certain individuals who have assisted us with specific aspects of this work. First among these is Prof. Timothy Earle, whose support has been continuous and unwavering since the initial development of the proposal. Furthermore, he has provided us with numerous suggestions that have significantly enriched the text in multiple ways. We would also like to extend our particular gratitude to Prof. Jonathan Edmondson (York University), who carefully reviewed the manuscript and offered multiple invaluable observations that have served to improve the text and address various errors and imprecisions. We also want to thank the peer reviewers for their critical feedback, which has enriched the text in many ways.

Funding Information

This work was supported by the Ministerio de Ciencia e Innovación under Grant MICINN PID2022-142712NB-I00 *Paisajes irrigados, huertas y minifundios de época romana. Análisis de los agrosistemas intensivos y sus lógicas económicas y sociales*, and by the Autonomous Community of Madrid "Atracción de Talento" Grant 2021-5A/HUM-20947 Carpetania rustica. *Arqueología de los asentamientos campesinos romanos en el centro de la Península.*

Cambridge Elements

Ancient and Pre-modern Economies

Kenneth G. Hirth
The Pennsylvania State University

Ken Hirth's research focuses on the development of ranked and state-level societies in the New World. He is interested in political economy and how forms of resource control lead to the development of structural inequalities. Topics of special interest include: exchange systems, craft production, settlement patterns, and preindustrial urbanism. Methodological interests include: lithic technology and use-wear, ceramics, and spatial analysis.

Timothy Earle
Northwestern University

Timothy Earle is an economic anthropologist specializing in the archaeological studies of social inequality, leadership, and political economy in early chiefdoms and states. He has conducted field projects in Polynesia, Peru, Argentina, Denmark, and Hungary. Having studied the emergence of social complexity in three world regions, his work is comparative, searching for the causes of alternative pathways to centralized power.

Emily J. Kate
University of Vienna

Emily Kate is bioarchaeologist with training in radiocarbon dating, isotopic studies, human osteology, and paleodemography. Having worked with projects from Latin America and Europe, her interests include the manner in which paleodietary trends can be used to assess shifts in social and political structure, the affect of migration on societies, and the refinement of regional chronologies through radiocarbon programs.

About the Series

Elements in Ancient and Pre-modern Economies is committed to critical scholarship on the comparative economies of traditional societies. Volumes either focus on case studies of well documented societies, providing information on domestic and institutional economies, or provide comparative analyses of topical issues related to economic function. Each Element adopts an innovative and interdisciplinary view of culture and economy, offering authoritative discussions of how societies survived and thrived throughout human history.

Cambridge Elements =

Ancient and Pre-modern Economies

Elements in the Series

Ancient and Pre-modern Economies of the North American Pacific Northwest
Anna Marie Prentiss

The Aztec Economy
Frances F. Berdan

Shell Money: A Comparative Study
Mikael Fauvelle

A Historical Ethnography of the Enga Economy of Papua New Guinea
Polly Wiessner, Akii Tumu and Nitze Pupu

Ancient Maya Economies
Scott R. Hutson

Nordic Bronze Age Economies
Christian Horn, Knut Ivar Austvoll, Magnus Artursson and Johan Ling

Economies of the Inca World
R. Alan Covey and Jordan Dalton

The Shang Economy
Roderick Campbell

Reading Creation Myths Economically in Ancient Mesopotamia and Israel
Eric J. Harvey

Peasant Economies and Societies in Ancient Roman Iberia
Jesús Bermejo Tirado and Ignasi Grau Mira

A full series listing is available at: www.cambridge.org/EAPE

Printed by Integrated Books International,
United States of America